THE
PHILOSOPHY OF ANCIENT INDIA

THE PHILOSOPHY OF ANCIENT INDIA

RICHARD GARBE

GYAN

Published by

GYAN

Gyan Publishing House
5, Ansari Road
Daryaganj, New Delhi-110002
Phone: 011-47034999, 9811692060
E-mail: books@gyanbooks.com

Distribution Network
gyanbooks.com
India, USA, Canada, UK, Australia

ISBN: 978-93-6920-502-8 (HB)

First Published, 1899

2nd Impression 2025

Printed at: Gyan Press, Delhi.

THE PHILOSOPHY OF ANCIENT INDIA
Author: RICHARD GARBE

THE PHILOSOPHY OF ANCIENT INDIA

THE PHILOSOPHY OF ANCIENT INDIA

BY

RICHARD GARBE

PROFESSOR IN THE UNIVERSITY OF T'IEBINGEN

SECOND EDITION

CHICAGO
THE OPEN COURT PUBLISHING COMPANY
LONDON AGENTS
KEGAN PAUL, TRENCH, TRUEBNER & CO.
1899

TABLE OF CONTENTS.

BRIEF OUTLINE OF A HISTORY OF INDIAN PHILOSOPHY.

A DISTINCTIVE leaning to metaphysical speculation is noticeable among the Indians from the earliest times. Old hymns of the Ṛigveda, which in other respects are still deeply rooted in the soil of polytheism, show already the inclination to comprehend multifarious phenomena as a unity, and may therefore be regarded as the first steps in the path which led the old Indian people to pantheism. Monotheistic ideas also occur in the later Vedic hymns, but are not developed with sufficient logic to displace the multiform world of gods from the consciousness of the people

The properly philosophical hymns, of which there are few in the Ṛigveda, and not many more in the Atharvaveda, belong to the latest products of the Vedic poetry. They concern themselves with the problem of the origin of the world, and with the eternal principle that creates and maintains the world, in obscure phraseology, and in unclear, self-contradictory trains of thought, as might be expected of the early beginnings of speculation. The Yajurvedas, also, contain remarkable and highly fantastic cosmogonic legends, in which the world-creator produces things by the all-powerful sacrifice. It is worthy of notice that the ideas of the portions of the Veda are intimately related with those of the earlier Upanishads, in fact in many respects are identical;[1] their connexion is also further evinced by the fact that both in these Upanishads and in the cosmogonic hymns and legends of the Veda the subjects discussed make their appearance absolutely without order. Still, the pre-Buddhistic Upanishads, and, in part, also their precursors, the Brâhmaṇas, which deal essentially with ritualistic questions, and the more speculative Âraṇyakas, are of the greatest importance for our studies; for they represent a time (beginning we know not when, and ending in the sixth century about) in which the ideas were developed that became determinative of the whole subsequent direction of Indian thought:[2] first and above all, the doctrine of the transmigration of souls, and the theory intimately connected therewith of the subsequent effects of actions (*karman*). The be-

[1] Compare on this point Lucian Scherman, *Philosophische Hymnen aus der Rig- und Atharva-Veda-Sanhitâ verglichen mit den Philosophemen der älteren Upanishads*, Strassburg-London, 1887.

[2] Compare A. E. Gough, *The Philosophy of the Upanishads and Ancient Indian Metaphysics*, London, 1882. The singular unfavorable judgment of the whole philosophy of the Upanishads which Gough pronounces in the opening of his otherwise valuable book, may perhaps be explained by the morbid aversion to all things Indian, which absorbing work so very frequently produces in Europeans dwelling any length of time in India.

lief that every individual unceasingly moves forward after death towards new existences in which it will enjoy the fruits of formerly won merits, and will suffer the consequences of formerly committed wrongs—whether in the bodies of men, animals, or plants, or in heavens and hells—has dominated the Indian people from that early period down to the present day. The idea was never made the subject of philosophical demonstration, but was regarded as something self-evident, which, with the exception of the Chârvâkas, or Materialists, no philosophical school or religious sect of India ever doubted.

The origin of the Indian belief in metempsychosis is unfortunately still shrouded in obscurity. In the old Vedic time a joyful view of life prevailed in India in which we discover no germs whatever of the conception which subsequently dominated and oppressed the thought of the whole nation ; as yet the nation did not feel life as a burden but as the supreme good, and its eternal continuance after death was longed for as the reward of a pious life. In the place of this innocent joy of life suddenly enters, without noticeable evidences of transition, the conviction that the existence of the individual is a journey full of torments from death to death. It is natural enough, therefore, to suspect foreign influence in this sudden revolution of thought.

I do not believe that Voltaire's rationalistic explanation of the origin of the Indian doctrine of the transmigration of souls now counts any adherents in professional circles ; but it is remarkable enough to merit a passing notice. According to the theory of the ingenious Frenchman the knowledge that the use of meat was upon the whole injurious to health in the climate of India was the ground of the prohibition to kill animals. This originally purely hygienic precept was clothed in religious trappings, and the people thus gradually grew accustomed to reverence and to worship animals. The consequence of the further extension of this animal cult then was, that the whole animal kingdom was felt as a sort of appurtenance to the human species and was gradually assimilated to man in the imagination of the people; from there it was simply a step to accept the continuance of human life in the bodies of animals. This whole hypothesis has long since been rejected, and also several subsequent attempts at explanation must be regarded as unsuccessful.

A suggestion of Gough (*The Philosophy of the Upanishads*, pp. 24–25) alone demands more serious consideration. It is well known that the belief that the human soul passes after death into the trunks of trees and the bodies of animals is extremely widespread among half-savage tribes.[1] On the basis of this fact,

[1] "The Sonthals are said to believe the souls of the good to enter into fruitbearing trees. The Powhattans believed the souls of their chiefs to pass into particular wood-birds, which they therefore spared. The Tlascalans of Mexico thought that the souls of their nobles migrated after death into beautiful singing-birds, and the spirits of plebeians into beetles, weasels, and other insignificant creatures. The Zulus of South Africa are said to believe the

Gough assumes that the Aryans, on their amalgamation with the original indigenous inhabitants of India, received from these the idea of the continuance of life in animals and trees. Although this assumption can hardly ever be made the subject of proof,[1] the idea, in my opinion, is very probable, because it explains what no other combinations do sufficiently explain. But we must be on our guard lest we overrate the influence of the crude conceptions of the aborigines. With all tribes low in the scale of civilisation the idea implied in such beliefs is not that of a transmigration of souls in the Indian sense, but simply the notion of a continuance of human existence in animals and trees; with this, reflexion on the subject reaches its goal; further consequences are not drawn from the idea. Under all circumstances, therefore, the Aryan Indians can have received only the first impetus to the development of the theory of transmigration from the aboriginal inhabitants; the elaboration of the idea they borrowed—the assumption of a *constant*, *changing* continuance of life, and its connexion with the doctrine of the power of deeds, having in view the satisfaction of the moral consciousness—must always be regarded as their own pe-

passage of the dead into snakes, or into wasps and lizards. The Dayaks of Borneo imagine themselves to find the souls of the dead, damp and bloodlike, in the trunks of trees." Gough, following Tylor, *Primitive Culture*, Vol. II., p. 6 et seq.

[1] One noteworthy passage bearing on this point may be found in Baudhâyana's Dharmaçâstra, II., 8. 14. 9, 10, where it is prescribed that dumplings of flour should be thrown to the birds, just as they are offered in the usual ancestral sacrifices; "for it is said that our ancestors hover about in the shape of birds."

culiar achievement. The dominating idea of this doctrine is the firm conviction that *unmerited* misfortune can befall no one. On the ground of this conviction an explanation was sought for the fact of daily observation that the bad fare well, and the good fare ill; that animals, and often even the new-born child, who have had no opportunity to incur guilt, must suffer the greatest agonies; and no other explanation was found than the assumption that in this life are expiated the good and bad deeds of a former existence. But what held true of that existence must also have held true of the one which preceded it; again the reason of formerly experienced happiness and misery could only be found in a preceding life. And thus there was no limit whatever to the existence of the individual in the past. The Saṃsâra, the cycle of life, has, therefore, no beginning; for "the work (that is, the conduct or actions) of beings is beginningless." But what has no beginning has by a universally admitted law also no end. The Saṃsâra, therefore, never ceases, no more than it never began. When the individual receives the rewards for his good and his bad deeds, a residuum of merit and guilt is always left which is not consumed and which demands its recompense or its punishment, and, therefore, still acts as the germ of a new existence. Unexpiated or unrewarded no deed remains; for "as among a thousand cows a calf finds its mother, so the previously done deed follows after the doer," says the Mahâbhârata, giving in words the view which had long since become in India the universal belief. Now, as the cause of all action is desire, desire was declared to be the motive power of the eternal continuance of life. Again, as desire was conceived by the Indian mind to have its root in a sort of ignorance, in a mistaking of the true nature and value of things, in ignorance, it was thought, the last cause of Saṃsâra was hidden. Equally as old is the conviction that the law which fetters living beings to the existence of the world *can* be broken. There is salvation from the Saṃsâra; and the means thereto is the saving knowledge, which is found by every philosophical school of India in some special form of cognition.

The dogmas here developed are summarised by Deussen, *System des Vedânta*, pp. 381–382, in the following appropriate words: "The idea is this, that life, in quality as well as in quantity, is the precisely meted, absolutely appropriate expiation of the deeds of the previous existence. This expiation is accomplished by *bhoktṛitvam* and *kartṛitvam* (enjoying and acting), where the latter again is converted into works which must be expiated afresh in a subsequent existence, so that the clock-work of atonement in running down always winds itself up again; and this unto all eternity —unless the universal knowledge appears which . . . . does not rest on merit but breaks into life without connexion with it, to dissolve it in its innermost elements, to burn up the seeds of works, and thus to make impossible for all future time a continuance of the transmigration."

What Deussen here expounds as a doctrine of the Vedânta system is a body of ideas which belongs alike to all systems of Brahman philosophy and to Buddhism and Jinism. But the power which inheres in the actions of beings extends, according to the Indian idea, still farther than was stated in the preceding exposition. This subsequent effectiveness of guilt and of merit, usually called *adrishta*, "the invisible," also often simply *karman*, "deed, work," not only determines the measure of happiness and suffering which falls to the lot of each individual, but also determines the origin and evolution of all things in the universe. At bottom this last thought is only a necessary consequence of the theory that every being is the architect of its own fate and fortunes into the minutest details; for whatever comes to pass in the world, some creature is inevitably affected by it and must, therefore, by the law of atonement have brought about the event by his previous acts. The operations of nature, therefore, are the effects of the good and bad actions of living beings. When trees bear fruits, or the grain of the fields ripens, the power which is the cause of this, according to the Indian, is human merit.

Even in the systems which accept a God, the sole office of the Deity is to guide the world and the fates of creatures in strict agreement with the law of retribution, which even he cannot break. For the many powers to which the rest of the world, orthodox and unorthodox, ascribe a determinative influence on the lot of individuals and nations as also on the control of the forces of nature,—divine grace and punishment, the order of the world, foresight, fate, accident—in India there is no place by the side of the power of the work or deed which rules all with iron necessity. On these assumptions all Indian philosophy, with the exception of materialism, is founded.

The most important theme of the early Upanishads, which stand at the head of the real philosophical literature of India, is the question of the Eternal One. It is true, those works abound in reflexions on theological, ritualistic, and other matters, but all these reflexions are utterly eclipsed by the doctrine of the Eternal One, the *Âtman* or *Brahman*. The word Âtman originally meant "breathing," then "the vital principle," "the Self"; but soon it was used to signify the Intransient ONE which is without any attribute or quality,—the All-Soul, the Soul of the world, the Thing-in-itself, or whatever you like to translate it. Brahman, on the other hand, originally "the prayer," became a term for the power which is inherent in every prayer and holy action, and at last for the eternal, boundless power which is the basis of everything existing. Having attained this stage of development, the word Brahman became completely synonymous with Âtman. The objective Brahman and the subjective Âtman amalgamated into one, the highest metaphysical idea; and this amalgamation comprises the doctrine of the unity of the subject and the object. In numerous parables the Upanishads try to describe the nature of Brahman, but all their reflexions culminate in one point: the inmost Self of the individual being is one with that all-pervading power (*tat tvam asi*, "thou art That").

This spiritual monism challenged the contradiction of Kapila, the founder of the Sâṃkhya philosophy,[1] who, in a rationalistic way, saw only the diversity, but not the unity of the universe. The Sâṃkhya doctrine—the oldest real system of Indian philosophy—is entirely dualistic. Two things are admitted, both eternal and everlasting, but in their innermost character totally different; namely, matter and soul, or better a boundless plurality of individual souls. The existence of the creator and ruler of the universe is denied. The world develops according to certain laws out of primitive matter, which first produces those subtile substances of which the internal organs of all creatures are formed, and after that brings forth the gross matter. At the end of a period of the universe the products dissolve by retrogradation into primitive matter; and this continual cycle of evolution, existence, and dissolution has neither beginning nor end. The psychology of this interesting system is of special importance. All the functions which ordinarily we de-

[1] An exhaustive exposition of the doctrines of this system has been given by the author in his work on the Saṃkhya Philosophy, Leipsic, 1894, H. Haessel.

note as psychic, i. e., perception, sensation, thinking, willing, etc., according to the Sâṃkhya doctrine, are merely mechanical processes of the internal organs, that is, of matter. These would remain unconscious, if it were not for the soul which "illuminates" them, i. e., makes them conscious. No other object is accomplished by soul. Soul is perfectly indifferent and, therefore, also not the vehicle of moral responsibility. This office is assumed by the subtile or internal body, which is chiefly formed of the inner organs and the senses, and which surrounds the soul. This internal body accompanies soul from one existence into another, and is, therefore, the real principle of metempsychosis. It is the object of the Sâṃkhya philosophy to teach people to know the absolute distinction between soul and matter in its most subtile modifications, as it appears in the inner organs. A man has attained the highest aim of human exertion if this distinction is perfectly clear to him: discriminative knowledge delivers soul from the misery of the endless flow of existence and abolishes the necessity of being born again. The Sâṃkhya philosophy is already saturated with that pessimism which has put its stamp on the outcomes of this system.

The Sâṃkhya system supplied, in all main outlines, the foundations of Jinism and Buddhism, two philosophically embellished religions, which start from the idea that this life is nothing but suffering, and always revert to that thought. According to them the cause of suffering is the desire to live and to enjoy the delights of the world, and in the last instance the "ignorance" from which this desire proceeds; the means of the abolition of this ignorance, and there-with of suffering, is the annihilation of that desire, renunciation of the world, and a most boundless exercise of practical love towards all creatures. In the subsequent time, it is true, Buddhism and Jinism so developed that some of their teachings were stoutly contested in the Sâṃkhya writings.[1] These two pessimistic religions are so extraordinarily alike that the Jains, that is, the adherents of Jina, were for a long time regarded as a Buddhistic sect, until it was discovered that the founders of the two religions were contemporaries, who in turn are simply to be regarded as the most eminent of the numerous teachers who in the sixth century before Christ in North Central India opposed the ceremonial doctrines and the caste-system of the Brahmans. The true significance of these religions lies in their high development of ethics, which in the scholastic Indian philosophy is almost

[1] One question here was of the doctrine of the Jains that the soul has the same extension as the body—a thought which is refuted by the argument that everything bounded is perishable, and that this would hold good with all the more force of the soul, as this in its transmigration through different bodies must be assimilated to the bodies that receive it, that is, must expand and contract, a feat achievable only by a thing made up of parts. But the main points attacked are the following views of Buddhism. The Sâṃkhyas principally impugn the Buddhistic denial of the soul as a compact, persistent principle, further the doctrine that all things possess only a momentary existence, and that salvation is the annihilation of self. From this it is plain that the Sâṃkhyas of the later epoch saw in Buddhism, which nevertheless was essentially an outgrowth of its system, one of its principal opponents.

wholly neglected. Buddhism and Jinism agree, however, with the latter, in the promise, made by all real systems of India, to redeem man from the torments of continued mundane life, and in their perception of a definite ignorance as the root of all mundane evil; but in the philosophical establishment of their principles, both method and clearness of thought are wanting.[1]

It must also be mentioned in this connexion that the religions of Buddha and Jina have as little broken with the mythological views of the people as the Brahmanic philosophical systems. The existence of gods, demigods, and demons is not doubted, but is of little importance. It is true the gods are more highly organised and more fortunate beings than men, but like these they also stand within the Saṃsâra, and if they do not acquire the saving knowledge and thus withdraw from mundane existence, must also change their bodies as soon as the power of their formerly won merit is exhausted. They, too, have not escaped the power of death, and they therefore stand lower than the man who has attained the highest goal.[2] Much easier than the attainment of this goal is it to lift oneself by virtue and good works to the divine

[1] Compare especially the Buddhistic formula of the causal nexus in Oldenberg's *Buddha*, Part II., Chapter 2.

[2] This belief in developed, ephemeral gods has nothing to do with the question of the eternal God accepted in some systems. The use of a special word (*Içvara*, "the powerful") in the Indian philosophy plainly grew out of the endeavor to distinguish verbally between *this* god and the popular gods *deva*.

plane, and to be born again after death on the moon or in the world of Indra or of Brahman, etc., even in the person of one of these gods; but only foolish men yearn after such transitory happiness.

In the second century before Christ the Yoga philosophy was founded by Patañjali. In part, this event is simply the literary fixation of the views which were held on asceticism and on the mysterious powers which it was assumed could be acquired by asceticism. The Yoga, that is, the turning away of the senses from the external world, and the concentration of the mind within, was known and practised many centuries previously in India. In the Buddhistic communion, for example, the state of ecstatic abstraction was always a highly esteemed condition. Patañjali, now, elaborated the doctrine of concentration into a system and described at length the means of attaining that condition, and of carrying it to its highest pitch. The methodical performance of the Yoga practice, according to Patañjali, leads not only to the possession of the supernatural powers, but is also the most effective means of attaining the saving knowledge.

The metaphysical basis of the Yoga system is the Sâṃkhya philosophy, whose doctrines Patañjali so completely incorporated into his system that that philosophy is with justice uniformly regarded in Indian literature as a branch of the Sâṃkhya. At bottom, all that Patañjali did was to embellish the Sâṃkhya system with the Yoga practice, the mysterious powers, and the personal god; his chief aim had, no doubt, been to render this system acceptable to his fellow-countrymen by the eradication of its atheism. But the insertion of the personal god, which subsequently decisively determined the character of the Yoga system, was, to judge from the Yogasûtras, the text-book of Patañjali, at first accomplished in a very loose and superficial manner, so that the contents and purpose of the system were not at all affected by it. We can even say that the Yogasûtras I. 23–27, II. 1, 45, which treat of the person of God, are unconnected with the other parts of the text-book, nay, even contradict the foundations of the system. The ultimate goal of human aspiration according to that text-book is not union with or absorption in God, but exactly what it is in the Sâṃkhya philosophy, the absolute isolation (*kaivalya*) of the soul from matter. When L. von Schroeder (*Indiens Literatur und Cultur*, p. 687) says: "The Yoga bears throughout a theistic character; it assumes a primitive soul from which the individual souls proceed," his statement is incorrect, for the individual souls are just as much beginningless as the "special soul" (*purusha-viçesha*, Yogasûtra, I. 24) that is called God.

In contrast to these two closely related systems, Sâṃkhya and Yoga, the ancient, genuine Brahmanic elements, the ritual and the idealistic speculation of the Upanishads, are developed in a methodical manner in the two following intimately connected systems whose origin we can place approximately at the beginning of the Christian era.

The Pûrva-(or Karma)mîmâṃsâ, "the first inquiry," or "the inquiry concerning works," usually briefly called Mîmâṃsâ, founded by Jaimini, is probably counted among the philosophical systems only because of its form and its connexion with the Vedânta doctrine; for it is concerned with the interpretation of the Veda, which it holds to be uncreated and existent from all eternity: classifying its component parts and treating of the rules for the performance of the ceremonies, as of the rewards which singly follow upon the latter. This last is the main theme of this system, in which the true scriptural scholarship of the Brahmans is condensed. Questions of general significance are only incidentally discussed in the Mîmâṃsa. Especial prominence belongs here to the proposition that the articulate sounds are eternal, and to the theory based upon it, that the connexion of a word with its significance is independent of human agreement, and, consequently, that the significance of a word is inherent in the word itself, by nature. Hitherto, the Mîmâṃsa has little occupied the attention of European indologists; the best description of its principal contents will be found in the "Introductory Remarks" of G. Thibaut's edition of the Arthasaṃgraha (*Benares Sanskrit Series*, 1882).

The Uttara-(or Brahma-)mîmâṃsa, "the second inquiry," or "the inquiry into the Brahman," most commonly called Vedânta, bears some such relation to the earlier Upanishads as, to use an expression of Deussen's, Christian dogmatics bear to the New Testament. Its founder, Bâdarâyaṇa, accepted and further developed the above-discussed doctrines of the Brahman-Âtman, into the system which to the present day determines the world-view of the Indian thinkers. This system has received excellent and exhaustive treatment in the above-cited work of Deussen, which is to be emphatically recommended to all interested in Indian philosophy. The basis of the Vedânta is the principle of the identity of our Self with the Brahman. Since, now, the eternal, infinite Brahman is not made up of parts, and cannot be subject to change, consequently our self is not a part or emanation of it, but is the whole, indivisible Brahman. Other being besides this there is not, and, accordingly, the contents of the Vedânta system are comprehended in the expression *advaita-vâda*, "the doctrine of non-duality." The objection which experience and the traditional belief in the transmigration of souls and in retribution raise against this principle, has no weight with Bâdarâyaṇa; experience and the doctrine of retribution are explained by the ignorance (*avidyâ*), inborn in man, which prevents the soul from discriminating between itself, its body and organs, and from recognising the empirical world as an illusion (*mâyâ*). The Vedânta philosophy does not inquire into the reason and origin of this ignorance; it simply teaches us that it exists and that it is annihilated by knowledge (*vidyâ*), that is, by the universal knowledge which grasps the illusory nature of all that is not soul, and the absolute identity of the soul with the Brahman. With this knowledge, the conditions of the continuance of the mundane existence of the soul are removed—for this in truth is only semblance and illusion—and salvation is attained.

In this way are the Brahmasûtras, the text-book of Bâdarâyaṇa, expounded by the famous exegetist Çaṃkara (towards 800 after Christ), upon whose commentary Deussen's exposition is based. Now, as this text-book, like the chief works of the other schools, is clothed in the form of aphorisms not intelligible *per se*, we are unable to prove from its simple verbal tenor that Çaṃkara was always right in his exegesis; but intrinsic reasons render it in the highest degree probable that the expositions of Çaṃkara agree in all essential points with the system which was laid down in the Brahmasûtras. The subsequent periods produced a long succession of other commentaries on the Brahmasûtras, which in part give expression to the religio-philosophical point of view of special sects. The most important of these commentaries is that of Râmânuja, which dates from the first half of the twelfth century. Râmânuja belonged to one of the oldest sects of India, the Bhâgavatas or Pâñcharâtras, who professed an originally un-Brahmanic, popular monotheism, and saw salvation solely in the love of God (*bhakti*). Upon the Brahmanisation of this sect, their God (usually called Bhagavant or Vâsudeva) was identified with Vishṇu, and from that time on the Bhâgavatas are considered as a Vishṇuitic sect. Its doctrine, which is closely related to Christian ideas, but, in my opinion, was not constructed under Christian influences, is chiefly expounded in the Bhagavadgîtâ, in the Çâṇḍilyasûtras, in the Bhâgavata Purâṇa, and in the textbooks proper of the sect, among which we may also reckon Râmânuja's commentary on the Brahmasûtras. According to the tenet of the Bhâgavatas, the individual souls are not identical with the highest soul or God, and are also not implicated by a kind of "ignorance" in mundane existence, but by unbelief. Devout love of God is the means of salvation, that is, of union with the Highest. The best exposition of the system which Râmânuja imported into the Brahmasûtras will be found in R. G. Bhandarkar's *Report on the Search for Sanskrit Manuscripts During the Year 1883–1884*, Bombay, 1887, p. 68 et seq.

As of the systems thus far considered always two are found intimately connected, the Sâṃkhya-Yoga on the one hand and the Mîmâṃsâ-Vedânta on the other, so also in a subsequent period the two remaining systems which passed as orthodox, the Vaiçeshika and the Nyâya, were amalgamated. The reason of this was manifestly the circumstance that both inculcated the origin of the world from atoms and were signalised by a sharp classification of ideas; yet the

Vaiçeshika system is certainly of much greater antiquity than the Nyâya. The former is already attacked in the Brahmasûtras, II., 2, 12–17, where at the conclusion the interesting remark is found that it is unworthy of consideration because no one embraced it. But in a subsequent period the system, far from being despised, became very popular.

Kaṇâda (Kaṇabhuj or Kaṇabhaksha) is considered the founder of the Vaiçeshika system; but this name, which signifies etymologically "atom-eater," appears to have been originally a nickname suggested by the character of the system; but which ultimately supplanted the true name of the founder.

The strength of the system is contained in its enunciation of the categories, under which, as Kaṇâda thought, everything that existed might be subsumed: substance, quality, motion (or action), generality, particularity, and inherence. These notions are very sharply defined and broken up into subdivisions. Of especial interest to us is the category of inherence or inseparability (*samavâya*). This relation, which is rigorously distinguished from accidental, soluble connexion (*saṃyoga*), exists between the thing and its properties, between the whole and its parts, between motion and the object in motion, between species and genus.

Later adherents of the Vaiçeshika system added to the six categories a seventh, which has exercised a momentous influence on the development of logical inquiries: non-existence (*abhâva*). With Indian subtlety this category also is divided into subspecies, namely into prior and posterior, mutual and absolute non-existence. Putting it positively, we should say, instead of "prior non-existence," "future existence," instead of "posterior non-existence," "past existence." "Mutual" or "reciprocal non existence" is that relation which obtains between two non-identical things (for example, the fact that a jug is not a cloth, and *vice versa*); "absolute non-existence" is illustrated by the example of the impossibility of fire in water.

Now, Kaṇâda by no means limited himself to the enunciation and specialisation of the categories. He takes pains, in his discussion of them, to solve the most various problems of existence and of thought, and thus to reach a comprehensive philosophical view of the world. The category substance, under which notion, according to him, earth, water, light, air, ether, time, space, soul, and the organ of thought fall, affords him the occasion of developing his theory of the origin of the world from atoms; the category quality, in which are embraced besides the properties of matter also the mental properties: cognition, joy, pain, desire, aversion, energy, merit, guilt, and disposition, leads him to the development of his psychology and to the exposition of his theory of the sources of knowledge.

The psychological side of this system is very remarkable and exhibits some analogies with the corresponding views of the Sâṃkhya philosophy. The soul, according to Kaṇâda, is beginningless, eternal, and all-pervading, that is, limited neither by time nor space. If, now, the soul could come into immediate connexion with the objects of knowledge, all objects would reach consciousness simultaneously. That this is not the case, Kaṇâda explains by the assumption of the organ of thought or inner sense (*manas*), with which the soul stands in the most intimate connexion. The soul knows by means of this *manas* alone, and it perceives through it not only the external things, but also its own qualities. The *manas*, as contradistinguished from the soul, is an *atom*, and as such only competent to comprehend one object in each given instant.

The last of the six Brahmanic systems, the Nyâya philosophy of Gotama, is a development and complement of the doctrines of Kaṇâda. Its special significance rests in its extraordinarily exhaustive and acute exposition of formal logic, which has remained untouched in India down to the present day, and serves as the basis of all philosophical studies. The doctrine of the means of knowledge (perception, inference, analogy, and trustworthy evidence), of syllogisms, fallacies, and the like, is treated with the greatest fulness. The importance which is attributed to logic in the Nyâya system appears from the very first Sûtra of Gotama's text-book in which sixteen logical notions are enumerated with the remark that the attainment of the highest salvation depends upon a correct knowledge of their nature. The psychology of the Nyâya agrees fully with that of the Vaiçeshika system. The metaphysical foundations, too, are the same here as in that system; in both, the world is conceived as an agglomeration of eternal, unalterable, and causeless atoms. The fundamental text-books of the two schools, the Vaiçeshika and Nyâya Sûtras, originally did not accept the existence of God; it was not till a subsequent period that the two systems changed to theism, although neither ever went so far as to assume a creator of matter. Their theology is first developed in Udayanâchârya's Kusumâñjali (towards 1300 after Christ), as also in the works which treat jointly of the Nyâya and Vaiçeshika doctrines. According to them, God is a special soul, like all other individual and similarly eternal souls, only with the difference that to him those qualities are wanting that condition the transmigration of the other souls, or that are conditioned by that transmigration (merit, guilt, aversion, joy, pain), and that he alone possesses the special attributes of omnipotence and omniscience, by which he is made competent to be the guide and regulator of the universe.

In the first centuries after Christ an *eclectic* movement, which was chiefly occupied with the combination of the Sâṃkhya, Yoga, and Vedânta theories, was started in India. The oldest literary production of this movement is the Çvetâçvatara Upanishad. composed by a Çivite, the supreme being in this Upanishad being invested with the name of Çiva. More celebrated than this Upanishad is the Bhagavadgîtâ, admired equally in India and in the Occident for its loftiness of thought and expression—an episode of the Mahâbhârata. In the Bhagavadgîtâ, the supreme being appears incarnated in the person of Kṛishṇa, who stands at the side of the famous bowman, Arjuna, as his charioteer, expounding to this personage shortly before the beginning of a battle his doctrines. Nowhere in the philosophical and religious literature of India are the behests of duty so beautifully and strongly emphasised as here. Ever and anon does Kṛishṇa revert to the doctrine, that for every man, no matter to what caste he may belong, the zealous performance of his duty and the discharge of his obligations is his most important work.

The six systems Mîmâṃsâ, Vedânta, Sâṃkhya, Yoga, Vaiçeshika, and Nyâya, are accepted as orthodox (*âstika*) by the Brahmans; but the reader will notice, that in India this term has a different significance from what it has with us. In that country, not only has *the most absolute freedom of thought* always prevailed, but also philosophical speculation, even in its boldest forms, has placed itself in accord with the popular religion to an extent never again realised on earth between these two hostile powers. One concession only the Brahman caste demanded; the recognition of its class-prerogatives and of the infallibility of the Veda. Whoever agreed to this passed as orthodox, and by having done so assured for his teachings much greater success than if he had openly proclaimed himself a heretic (*nâstika*) by a refusal of such recognition. The concession demanded by the Brahmans, so far as it referred to Scripture, needed only to be a nominal one; it compelled neither full agreement with the doctrines of the Veda, nor the confession of any belief in the existence of God.

By the side of the Brahmanic and non-Brahmanic systems mentioned in this survey, we find also in India that view of the world which is "as old as philosophy itself, but not older":[1] materialism. The Sanskrit word for "materialism" is *lokâyata* ("directed to the world of sense"), and the materialists are called *lokâyatika* or *laukâyatika*, but are usually named, after the founder of their theory, Chârvâkas. Several vestiges show that even in pre-Buddhistic India proclaimers of purely materialistic doctrines appeared; and there is no doubt that those doctrines had ever afterwards, as they have to-day, numerous secret followers. Although one source (Bhâskarâchârya on the Brahmasûtra III. 3. 53) attests the *quondam* existence of a text-book of materialism, the Sûtras of Bṛihaspati (the mythical founder), yet in all India materialism found no other literary expression. We are referred, therefore, for an understanding of that philosophy, principally to the polemics which were directed against it in the text-books of the other philosophical

[1] The first words of Lange's *History of Materialism*.

schools, and to the first chapter of the Sarva-darçana-saṃgraha, a compendium of all philosophical systems, compiled in the fourteenth century by the well-known Vedântic teacher Mâdhavâchârya (translated into English by Cowell and Gough, London, 1882,) in which the system is expounded. Mâdhavâchârya begins his exposition with an expression of regret that the majority of mankind espouse the materialism represented by Chârvâka.

Another Vedântic teacher, Sadânanda, speaks in his Vedântasâra, §§ 148–151, of four materialistic schools, which are distinguished from one another by their conception of the soul; according to the first, the soul is identical with the gross body, according to the second, with the senses, according to the third, with the breath, and according to the fourth, with the organ of thought or the internal sense (*manas*). No difference in point of principle exists between these four views; for the senses, the breath, and the internal organ are really only attributes or parts of the body. Different phases of Indian materialism are, accordingly, not to be thought of.

The Chârvâkas admit perception only as a means of knowledge, and reject inference. As the sole reality they consider the four elements; that is, matter. When through the combination of the elements, the body is formed, then by their doctrine the soul also is created exactly as is the power of intoxication from the mixture of certain ingredients. With the annihilation of the body, the soul also is annihilated. The soul, accordingly, is nothing but the body with the attribute of intelligence, since soul different from the body cannot be established by sense-perception. Naturally, all other supra-sensual things also are denied, and in part treated with irony. Hell is earthly pain produced by earthly causes. The highest being is the king of the land, whose existence is proved by the perception of the whole world; salvation is the dissolution of the body. The after effects of merit and of guilt, which by the belief of all other schools determine the fate of every individual in its minutest details, do not exist for the Chârvâka, because this idea is reached only by inference. To the animadversion of an orthodox philosopher that the varied phenomena of this world have no cause for him who denies this all-powerful factor, the Chârvâka retorts, that the true nature of things is the cause from which the phenomena proceed.

The practical side of this system is eudæmonism of the crudest sort; for sensuous delight is set up as the only good worth striving for. The objection that sensuous pleasures cannot be the highest goal of man because a certain measure of pain is always mingled with them, is repudiated with the remark that it is the business of our intelligence to enjoy pleasures in the purest form possible, and to withdraw ourselves as much as possible from the pain inseparably connected with them. The man who wishes fish takes their scales and bones into the bargain, and he who wishes rice takes its stalks. It is absurd, therefore, for fear of pain, to give up pleasure, which we instinctively feel appeals to our nature.

The Vedas are stigmatised as the gossip of knaves, infected with the three faults of falsehood, self-contradiction, and useless tautology, and the advocates of Vedic science are denounced as cheats whose doctrines annul one another. For the Chârvâkas, the Brahmanic ritual is a swindle, and the costly and laborious sacrifices serve only the purpose of procuring for the rogues who perform them a subsistence. "If an animal sacrificed gets into heaven, why does not the sacrificer rather slay his own father?" No wonder that for the orthodox Indian the doctrine of the Chârvâkas is the worst of all heresies. The text-books of the orthodox schools seek, as was said above, to refute this dangerous materialism. As an example, we may cite the refutation of the doctrine that there is no means of knowledge except perception, given in the Sâṃkhya-tattva-kaumudî, § 5, where we read: "When "the materialist affirms that 'inference is not a means "of knowledge,' how is it that he can know that a "man is ignorant, or in doubt, or in error? For truly "ignorance, doubt, and error cannot possibly be dis-"covered in other men by sense-perception. Accord-"ingly, even by the materialist, ignorance, etc., in "other men must be inferred from conduct and from "speech, and, therefore, inference is recognised as a "means of knowledge even against the materialist's "will."

Besides the systems here briefly reviewed, the above-mentioned Sarva-darçana-saṃgraha enumerates six more schools, which on account of their subordinate importance and their not purely philosophical character may be passed over in this survey. There is question first of a Vishṇuitic sect founded by Ânandatîrtha (or Pûrṇaprajña), and secondly of four Çivite sects, the names of whose systems are Nakulîça-Pâçupata, Çaiva, Pratyabhijñâ, and Raseçvara. The doctrines of these five sects are strongly impregnated with Vedantic and Sâṃkhya tenets. The sixth system is that of Pâṇini, that is grammatical science, which is ranked in Mâdhava's Compendium among the philosophies, because the Indian grammarians accepted the dogma of the eternity of sound taught in the Mîmâṃsâ, and because they developed in a philosophical fashion a theory of the Yoga system, namely the theory of the Sphoṭa, or the indivisible, unitary factor latent in every word as the vehicle of its significance.

If we pass in review the plenitude of the attempts made in India to explain the enigmas of the world and of our existence, the Sâṃkhya philosophy claims our first and chief attention, because it alone attempts to solve its problems solely by the means of reason. The genuinely philosophical spirit in which its method is manipulated of rising from the known factors of experience to the unknown by the path of logical demonstration, thus to reach a knowledge of the final cause, is acknowledged with admiration by all inquirers who have seriously occupied themselves with this system. In Kapila's doctrine, for the first time in the history of the world, the complete independence and freedom of the human mind, its full confidence in its own powers were exhibited. Although John Davies (Sānkhya Kārikā, p. V) slightly exaggerates matters when he says "The system of Kapila . . . . contains nearly all that India has produced in the department of pure philosophy," yet Kapila's system may claim, more than any other product of the fertile Indian mind, the interest of those contemporaries whose view of the world is founded on the results of modern physical science.

As for those who feel inclined to look down slightingly from a monistic point of view upon a dualistic conception of the world, the words of E. Rōer in the Introduction of the Bhâshâpariccheda, p. XVI, may be quoted: "Though a higher development of philosophy may destroy the distinctions between soul "and matter, that is, may recognise matter, or what "is perceived as matter, as the same with the soul (as "for instance, Leibniz did), it is nevertheless certain "that no true knowledge of the soul is possible without first drawing a most decided line of demarcation between the phenomena of matter and of the "soul." This sharp line of demarcation between the two domains was first drawn by Kapila. The knowledge of the difference between body and soul is one condition, and it is also an indispensable condition, of arriving at a true monism. Every view of the world which confounds this difference can supply at best a one-sided henism, be it a spiritualism or an equally one-sided materialism.

THE CONNEXION BETWEEN INDIAN AND GREEK PHILOSOPHY.

THE coincidences between Indian and Greek philosophy are so numerous that some of them were noticed immediately after the Indian systems became known to Europeans.

The most striking resemblance—I am almost tempted to say sameness—is that between the doctrine of the All-One in the Upanishads and the philosophy of the Eleatics. Xenophanes teaches that God and the Universe are one, eternal, and unchangeable; and Parmenides holds that reality is due alone to this universal being, neither created nor to be destroyed, and omnipresent; further, that everything which exists in multiplicity and is subject to mutability is not real; that thinking and being are identical. All these doctrines are congruent with the chief contents of the Upanishads and of the Vedânta system, founded upon the latter. Quite remarkable, too, in Parmenides and in the Upanishads is the agreement in style of presentation; in both we find a lofty, forceful, graphical mode of expression and the employment of verse to this end. It is true, the ideas about the illusive character of the empirical world and about the identity between existence and thought are not yet framed into doctrines in the older Upanishads; we only find them in works which doubtlessly are later than the time of Xenophanes and Parmenides. But ideas from which those doctrines must ultimately have developed, are met with in the oldest Upanishads; for it is there that we find particular stress laid upon the singleness and immutability of Brahman and upon the identity of thought (*vijṅâna*) and Brahman. I therefore do not consider it an anachronism to trace the philosophy of the Eleatics to India.

But even earlier than this can analogies between the Greek and Indian Worlds of thought be traced. Thales, the father of the Grecian philosophy, imagines everything to have sprung from water. This certainly reminds us of a mythological idea which was very familiar to the Indians of the Vedic time; namely, the idea of the primeval water out of which the universe was evolved. Even in the oldest works of the Vedic literature there are numerous passages in which this primeval water is mentioned, either producing itself all things or being the matter out of which the Creator produces them.

Fundamental ideas of the Sâṃkhya philosophy, too, are found among the Greek physiologers. Anaximander assumes, as the foundation (ἀρχή) of all things, a primitive matter, eternal, unfathomable and indefinite, the *ἄπειρον*, from which the definite substances arise and into which they return again. If you now advert to the Sâṃkhya doctrine, that the material world is produced by Prakriti, the primitive matter, and, when the time has come, sinks back into it, the analogy is evident. Likewise the idea of an infinite succession of worlds and of natural opposites is common to Anaximander and the Sâṃkhya philosophy. Let us proceed to another example. There is Heraclitus, the "dark Ephesian," whose doctrine, it is true, touches Iranian ideas in its main points. Nevertheless it offers several parallels with the views of the Sâṃkhya philosophy. The *πάντα ῥεῖ* of Heraclitus is a suitable expression for the incessant change of the empirical world, set down by the Sâṃkhya, and his doctrine of the innumerable annihilations and reformations of the Universe is one of the best known theories of the Sâṃkhya system.[1]

But let us turn to the physiologers of later times. The first with whom we have to deal is Empedocles, whose theories of metempsychosis and evolution may well be compared with the corresponding ideas of the Sâṃkhya philosophy. But most striking is the agreement between the following doctrine of his, "Nothing can arise which has not existed before, and nothing existing can be annihilated," and that most character-

[1] Colebrooke, *Miscellaneous Essays*, second edition, Vol. I, p. 437, discovers other analogies between the philosophy of Heraclitus and the Sâṃkhya doctrine.

istic one of the Sâṃkhya system about the beginningless and endless reality of all products (*sat-kâryavâda*), or—as we should put it—about the eternity and indestructibility of matter. Yet quite apart from this agreement in fundamental doctrine, Empedocles shows in general a surprising similarity to Indian character and Indian modes of view. I take the liberty to cite here the words which Tawney, with no desire of proving a direct dependence of Empedocles on India, uttered in the *Calcutta Review*, Vol. LXII., p. 79: "He "has made as near an approach as a Greek could "make to the doctrines of Hindu philosophy. Indeed "his personality was almost as much Hindu as Greek. "He was a priest, a prophet, and a physician; he "often was seen at magic rites and he was proved to "have worked mighty miracles. Even in his lifetime "he considered himself to have purified his soul by "devotion; to have purged away the impurities of his "birth; to have become in fact jîvanmukta (that is, "one liberated in lifetime)." In addition, Tawney points out the fact that there sprung up in Empedocles, from the belief in the transmigration of souls, a dislike to flesh as food.

A connexion may be traced between the dualism of Anaxagoras and that of the Sâṃkhya philosophy. And notwithstanding his atomism, which is certainly not derived from India,[1] even Democritus in the princi-

[1] For it is beyond doubt that the Indian atomistical systems, Vaiçeshika and Nyâya, were conceived a long time after Leucippus and Democritus.

ples of his metaphysics, which probably are rooted in the doctrines of Empedocles, reminds us of a Sâṃkhya tenet, which is in almost literal agreement with the following: "Nothing can rise from nothing."[1] The same is true of his conception of the gods. To Democritus they are not immortal, but only happier than men and longer-lived; and this is in perfect harmony with the position the gods occupy not only in the Sâṃkhya but in all Indian systems. According to Indian ideas, the gods are subject to metempsychosis like human beings, and they also must step down, when their store of merit, formerly acquired, is exhausted. Says Çaṃkara, the renowned Vedântist, in his commentary on the Brahmasûtra (I., 3, 28): "Words like 'Indra' mean only the holding of a certain office, as the word 'general' for instance; he who at the time occupies this post is called 'Indra.'"

The same ideas are met with in Epicurus, whose dependency upon Democritus must needs have brought about a resemblance. But also on matters of other kinds Epicurus has laid down principles which in themselves as well as in their arguments bear a remarkable resemblance to Sâṃkhya doctrines. Epicurus, in denying that the world is ruled by God, because this hypothesis would necessitate our investing the deity with attributes and functions that are incongruous with the idea of the divine nature, gives voice to a doctrine that is repeated by the Sâṃkhya teach-

[1] Comp. Sâṃkhyasûtra, I., 78.

ers with unfatiguing impressiveness. We also occasionally meet, in the systematic works of the Sâṃkhya philosophy, a favorite argumentative formula of Epicurus, "Everything could rise from everything then."

It is a question requiring the most careful treatment to determine whether the doctrines of the Greek philosophers, both those here mentioned and others, were really first derived from the Indian world of thought, or whether they were constructed independently of each other in both India and Greece, their resemblance being caused by the natural sameness of human thought. For my part, I confess I am inclined towards the first opinion, without intending to pass an apodictic decision. The book of Ed. Röth (*Geschichte unserer abendländischen Philosophie*, first edition 1846, second edition 1862), the numerous works of Aug. Gladisch, and the tract of C. B. Schlüter (*Aristoteles' Metaphysik eine Tochter der Sâṃkhya-Lehre des Kapila*, 1874)—all go too far in their estimation of Oriental influence and in the presentment of fantastical combinations; moreover, they are all founded upon a totally insufficient knowledge of the Oriental sources.[1]

[1] Compare also the treatise of Baron v. Eckstein, "Ueber die Grundlagen der Indischen Philosophie und deren Zusammenhang mit den Philosophemen der westlichen Völker," *Indische Studien*, II., 369–388. Even earlier than this, such questions were treated with astounding boldness. With a facility of conception peculiar to him, Sir William Jones (Works, quarto ed., 1799, I., 360, 361) perceived the following analogies: "Of the philosophical schools it will be sufficient here to remark that the first Nyâya seems analogous to the Peripatetic; the second, sometimes called Vaiçeshika, to the Ionic; the two Mîmânsâs, of which the second is often distinguished by the name of Vedânta, to the Platonic; the first Sânkhya, to the Italic; and the second or Pâtanjala, to the Stoic philosophy: so that Gautama corresponds with Aristotle; Ka-

Nevertheless, I consider them to contain a kernel of truth, although it can hardly be hoped that this kernel will ever be laid bare with scientific accuracy. The *historical possibility* of the Grecian world of thought being influenced by India through the medium of Persia must unquestionably be granted, and with it the possibility of the above-mentioned ideas being transferred from India to Greece. The connexions between the Ionic inhabitants of Asia Minor and those of the countries to the east of it were so various and numerous during the time in question that abundant occasion must have offered itself for the exchange of ideas between the Greeks and the Indians, then living in Persia.[1]

Add to this the Greek tradition that the greater part of the philosophers with whom we have dealt, Thales, Empedocles, Anaxagoras, Democritus, and others, undertook journeys, sometimes of considerable duration, into Oriental countries for the sake of making philosophical studies, and the probability of our

nâda, with Thales; Jaimini, with Socrates; Vyâsa, with Plato; Kapila, with Pythagoras; and Patanjali, with Zeno. But an accurate comparison between the Grecian and Indian schools would require a considerable volume."

[1] In Ueberweg's *Grundriss der Geschichte der Philosophie*, revised and edited by Heinze, sixth edition, I., 36, I am happy to find the following passage: "With much better reason we could suppose a considerable Oriental influence in the form of a direct communication of the older Grecian philosophers with Oriental nations." But I am sorry to say, I cannot concur with the opinion of the author, expressed on the same page, that a perfect and decisive solution of this problem might be expected from the progress of Oriental studies. For even the closest acquaintance with the Oriental systems and religions cannot do away with the alternative, before mentioned on page 37; and, with one single exception which I shall presently consider, the means for fixing the limits of these foreign influences upon the older Grecian philosophy are utterly wanting.

supposition that these Grecian philosophers acquired Indian ideas on Persian ground will be increased. But it cannot be denied that if they really did borrow foreign ideas, they well understood the art of impressing on them the stamp of the Grecian intellect.

Hitherto I have purposely omitted a name which is much more intimately connected with this question than the others I have mentioned. While, for the derivation of Indian ideas in the case of the Grecian physiologers, the Eleatics and Epicurus, I could only assume a *certain probability* in favor of my hypothesis, there seems to be no doubt about the dependence of Pythagoras upon Indian philosophy and science; and all the more so, as the Greeks themselves considered *his* doctrines as foreign. It was Sir William Jones (Works, 8vo ed., III., 236)[1] who first pointed out the analogies between the Sâṃkhya system and the Pythagorean philosophy, starting from the name of the Indian system, which is derived from the word *samkhyâ*, "number," and from the fundamental importance attached to number by Pythagoras. After Jones, Colebrooke (*Miscellaneous Essays*, second edition, I., 436–437) expressed with even more emphasis the idea that the doctrines of Pythagoras might be rooted in India. He says: ". . . . Adverting to what has come to us of the history of Pythagoras, I shall not hesitate to acknowledge an inclination to consider the Grecian to have been . . . . indebted to Indian instructors."

[1] See Colebrooke, *Miscellaneous Essays*, second edition, I., 241.

Colebrooke gives the reason for his opinion (*loc. cit.*, 441 et seq.) in the following passage, which seems to me to be sufficiently important to quote in full:

"It may be here remarked, by the way, that the Pythagoreans, and Ocellus in particular, distinguish as parts of the world, the heaven, the earth, and the interval between them, which they term lofty and aërial. . . . Here we have precisely the heaven, earth, and (transpicuous) intermediate region of the Hindus.

"Pythagoras, as after him Ocellus, peoples the middle or aërial region with demons, as heaven with gods, and the earth with men. Here again they agree precisely with the Hindus, who place the gods above, man beneath, and spiritual creatures, flitting unseen, in the intermediate region.

"Nobody needs to be reminded, that Pythagoras and his successors held the doctrine of metempsychosis, as the Hindus universally do the same tenet of transmigration of souls.

"They agree likewise generally in distinguishing the sensitive, material organ (*manas*) from the rational and conscious living soul (*jîvâtman*): θυμός and φρήν of Pythagoras; one perishing with the body, the other immortal.

"Like the Hindus, Pythagoras, with other Greek philosophers, assigned a subtle ethereal clothing to the soul apart from the corporeal part, and a grosser clothing to it when united with the body; the *sûkshma* (or *linga*) *çarira* and *sthûla çarira* of the Sánkhyas and the rest. . . . I should be disposed to conclude that the Indians were in this instance teachers rather than learners."

Wilson (*Quarterly Oriental Magazine*, IV., 11, 12, and *Sánkhya Kárikâ*, p. XI) only incidentally touches on the analogies pointed out by Jones and Colebrooke.

Barthélemy Saint-Hilaire goes a little more into detail regarding one point. He treats, in his *Premier Mémoire sur le Sânkhya* (Paris, 1852, pp. 512,

513, 521, 522), of Pythagoras's theory of metempsychosis, and he is right in observing that the greater probability is on the side of its Indian origin, and not on its Egyptian one. Further, Barthélemy finds Sâṃkhya ideas in Plato, in the "Phædon," "Phædrus," "Timaeus," and in the "Republic": "Les analogies sont assez nombreuses et assez profondes pour qu'il soit impossible de les regarder comme accidentelles" (p. 514). He points out that the ideas of redemption and bondage are doctrines both of Plato and of the Sâṃkhya philosophy, inasmuch as they denote the liberation of soul from matter and the confinement of soul by matter; and that the idea of metempsychosis is common to both, together with that of the beginningless and endless existence of the soul. On p. 521 Barthélemy then says that Plato, the great admirer of the Pythagorean school, took these doctrines from Pythagoras; but if we ask where Pythagoras obtained them, all the appearances are, in his opinion, in favor of India.[1]

The supposition that Pythagoras derived his theory of transmigration from India, was several times broached in older works besides.[2]

In a much more exhaustive and comprehensive

[1] One instance may be mentioned here which E. Röer (*Bibliotheca Indica*, Vol. XV., p. 91) pointed out, that the striking coincidence of the fine comparison found in the Katha Upanishad, "of the body with a car, the soul with the charioteer, the senses with the horses, the mind with the reins, etc." with the similar comparison in the Phædrus.

[2] See Lucian Scherman, *Materialien zur Geschichte der Indischen Visionsliteratur*, p. 26, note 1.

manner, but evidently without knowledge of his predecessors, Leopold von Schroeder has also treated this subject in an essay, *Pythagoras und die Inder*, (Leipsic, 1884), which, notwithstanding the contrary opinion of Professor Weber,[1] seems to me to be perfectly correct in its main points. From Schroeder's combinations it follows, that almost all the doctrines ascribed to Pythagoras, both religio-philosophical and mathematical, were current in India as early as the sixth century before Christ, and even previously. As the most important of these doctrines appear in Pythagoras without connexion or explanatory background, whilst in India they are rendered comprehensible by the intellectual life of the times, Schroeder conclusively pronounces India to be the birthplace of the Pythagorean ideas. Of course, no power of conviction would rest in *single* traits of agreement;—and for that reason I did not venture to give any definite opinion with regard to the dependence of the other philosophers mentioned on India;—but with Pythagoras, it is the *quantity* of coincidences that enforces conviction; and the more so, as the concordance is also to be noticed in insignificant and arbitrary matters which cannot well be expected to appear independently in two different places. Here I must refer to Schroeder's detailed argumentation and can only indicate the chief features which Pythagoras and the ancient Indians

[1] *Literarisches Centralblatt*, 1884, p. 1563–1565. Compare also "Die Griechen in Indien," *Sitzungsberichte der Kgl. Preussischen Akademie der Wissenschaften zu Berlin*, XXXVII., pp. 923–926.

have in common: the theory of the transmigration of souls, in which there is harmony here and there even in noticeable details, and which Pythagoras cannot have taken from Egypt for the simple reason that modern Egyptology teaches us, that—in spite of the well-known passage in Herodotus—the ancient Egyptians were not familiar with the doctrine of metempsychosis; further, the curious prohibition of eating beans, the *πρὸς ἥλιον τετραμμένον μὴ ὀμιχεῖν*; the doctrine of the *five* elements, i. e., the assumption of ether as the fifth element, which obtains in the Pythagorean school as well as everywhere in India; above all the so-called Pythagorean theorem, developed in the Çulvasûtras[1]; the irrational number $\sqrt{2}$; then the whole character of the religio-philosophical fraternity, founded by Pythagoras, which is analogous to the Indian orders of the time; and at last the mystical speculation, peculiar to the Pythagorean school, which bears a striking resemblance to the fantastical notions greatly in favor with the so-called Brâhmaṇa literature.

Schroeder proceeds with a few more analogies of lesser value and of doubtful nature, and finally he is certainly mistaken in the two following points.

[1] Weber's polemic against Schroeder's treatise is chiefly based on the fact that he underestimates the age of the Culvasûtras which describe the mensurations of the sacrificial compound that led to the discovery of the renowned tenet. The Culvasûtras are not appendages to the Crautasûtras, but integrant parts of the great ritual complexes, each of which has been composed by *one* author. The material, offered to us in the Culvasûtras, is of course still much older than these compendiums themselves.

First, he holds that Pythagoras acquired his knowledge in India itself,—an idea excluded at once by reference to the history of ancient traffic.[1] The only country in which Pythagoras could possibly have met his Indian teachers, is Persia, to which place I above found myself obliged to ascribe the eventual mediation between Indian ideas and the Greek physiologers and Eleatics. The other point is that of the connexion between the Pythagorean doctrine and the Sâṃkhya philosophy, supposed by Schroeder. It may be that Pythagoras acquired his knowledge of the theories of metempsychosis and of the five elements from adherents of the Sâṃkhya system; but *further* relations are not to be discovered. Schroeder[2] tries, on pp. 72–76, to bring the fundamental idea of the Pythagorean philosophy, that number is the essence of all things, into connexion with a *fictitious*, older form of the Sâṃkhya philosophy. He says p. 74: "To me it appears to be evident from the name Sâṃkhya, that number (*samkhyâ*) originally had a deciding, fundamental importance in this system, although the later system, the books of which appeared more than a thousand years after the pre-Buddhistic Sâṃkhya doctrine of Kapila, has effaced this characteristic trait and entirely lost it." In stating this, Schroeder has overlooked the fact that those Upanishads which are full of Sâṃkhya doctrines and which must be dated

[1] The Grecian tradition of Pythagoras having visited India did not arise before the Alexandrine time.

[2] As before him Sir William Jones; comp. p. 39 above.

only a few hundred years later than Buddha, are, in the passages in question, also wanting in what he calls the "original" characteristic trait, and that they are in harmony with that system which he calls the "later one." He himself declares this theory to be a very bold one, but in reality it is perfectly baseless. There is not the smallest particle of evidence for the hypothesis that there ever existed a Sâṃkhya system different from that of our sources, which acquired its name from the mania for enumeration peculiar to it. On the contrary, weighty reasons speak against the supposition that our system has undergone noticeable changes in the course of time. If ever we should try to fabricate some historical link between the Sâṃkhya system and the Pythagorean numeral philosophy, the following idea only could occur to us. The doctrines of Pythagoras: Number is the essence of things, the elements of numbers are to be considered as the elements of everything existing, the whole universe is harmony and number—these doctrines are unique in the history of human thought, and, if their meaning should be something else than "everything existing is ruled by the mathematical law," they might be regarded as unphilosophical. It therefore does not appear to me as a thing utterly beyond possibility, that those ideas took root in a misunderstanding of Pythagoras. It is possible that he misinterpreted the words of his Indian teacher: "The Sâṃkhya philosophy is named after the enumeration of the material principles" into: "Number is considered the essence of the material principles in the Sâṃkhya system." But this surely is nothing but a supposition.

It is Lassen who in his *Indische Alterthumskunde* denies every Indian influence upon Grecian philosophy in ante-Christian times, but adopts it (III., p. 379 et seq.) for the Christian Gnosticism and Neo-Platonism. As lively relations between Alexandria and India are sufficiently attested for this time, it is indeed impossible to doubt Indian influence upon the doctrines of the Gnostics and Neo-Platonists.

Let us first dwell upon Gnosticism. Lassen holds that the Indian elements in the Gnostic systems were derived from Buddhism which (in the secondary, modified form it had assumed at that time) undoubtedly exercised a considerable influence upon the intellectual life of Alexandria. This influence is most clearly perceptible in the ideas formed by the Gnostics about the many spiritual worlds and the numerous heavens. These ideas are certainly derived from the fantastical cosmogony of later Buddhism. But I do not admit the great importance which Lassen attributes to Buddhism in the formation of the Gnostic systems. It is my opinion that, in Lassen's expositions the Sâṃkhya philosophy does not get all that is due to it. If we keep it in mind that the centuries in which Gnosticism was developed—that is, the second and third century after Christ—are coincident with the period during which the Sâṃkhya philosophy flourished in India, many things will appear in a different light to us, than was the case with Lassen.[1] On p. 385 he establishes a connexion between the doctrines of Buddhism and the Gnostic contrast of soul and matter. But is it not more natural to remember here the ideas which form the foundation of the Sâṃkhya philosophy? Another point with which we have to deal is the identification of soul and light, met with among almost all Gnostics. Lassen has brought forward some remote and singular speculations from the misty and imaginative realm of later Buddhism, to make plausible the Buddhistic influence upon this Gnostic doctrine. I cannot say that this endeavor has been a successful one. How very simple and natural the idea appears with which a mere glance at the Sâṃkhya philosophy furnishes us! For there we are taught something which was evidently not known to Lassen; viz., that *the soul is light* (*prakâça*),[2] which means, that the mechanical processes of the internal organs are illuminated or made conscious by the soul. This idea of the Sâṃkhyas, that soul and light are the same, or—to put it otherwise—that the soul consists of light, we un-

[1] On the other hand, I must confess that I am unable to trace that resemblance between the Sâṃkhya philosophy and the doctrine of the Valentinians on the origin of matter, which is stated by Lassen on pp. 400, 401. The agreements of the Sâṃkhya system with that of the Ophites, collected by Lassen in the following pages, likewise appear to me open to doubt.

[2] Comp. Sâṃkhyasûtra, I., 145: "[Soul is] light, because the non-intellectual and light do not belong together," and VI., 50: "Being distinct from the non-intellectual, [soul] which has the nature of thought illuminates the non-intellectual." The commentator Vijñânabhikshu makes the following remark on the first passage: "The soul is in its essence light like the sun," etc.

doubtedly have to regard as the source of the similar idea of the Gnostics.

In regard to another point, Lassen (on pp. 384, 398 et seq.) has rightly acknowledged the influence of the Sâṃkhya philosophy upon Gnosticism. It was Ferd. Chr. Baur who even before him (in his work, *Die christliche Gnosis*, pp. 54, 158 et seq.) had noticed the remarkable agreement of the classification of men into the three classes of *πνευματικοί*, *ψυχικοί*, and *ὑλικοί*, peculiar to several Gnostics, with the Sâṃkhya doctrine of the three Guṇas. As I have entered in detail upon this theory in my book on the Sâṃkhya philosophy, I only wish to state here that in this system every individual is considered as appertaining to the sphere of one of the three powers, according as the luminous, serene, and joyful, or the passionate, fickle, and painful, or again the dark, motionless, and dull character predominates. There is also another interesting parallel to be found.[1] It is that between the Sâṃkhya doctrine according to which the Buddhi, Ahaṃkâra, and Manas, that is, the substrata of the psychic processes, have an independent existence during the first stages of the evolution of the universe, and the Gnostic tenet which allots personal existence to intellect, will, and so on. I am sure that those who are better acquainted with the Gnostic systems than I am, would be successful in finding some more points

[1] Mentioned by Fitz-Edward Hall in his translation of Nehemiah Nîlakantha S'âstrî Gore's *A Rational Refutation of the Hindu Philosophical Systems*, Calcutta, 1862, p. 84.

of contact, upon studying the doctrines of the Sâṃkhya philosophy in detail.

In passing to Neo-Platonism, we find that here Lassen has valued the influence of the Sâṃkhya doctrines to its full extent. The views of Plotinus (204–269 A. D.), the chief of the Neo-Platonists, are in part in perfect agreement with those of the Sâṃkhya system. The following sentences must be placed here: the soul is free from sorrows and passions, untouched by all affections; for the sufferings of the world belong to matter. By his philosophy Plotinus promises to deliver the world from misery, and this is the same purpose as that of the Sâṃkhya system which strives to lead men to discriminative knowledge and with it to redemption, that is to say, to absolute painlessness. Though all Brahman systems have made it their task to liberate mankind from the miseries of mundane existence by means of some special knowledge, yet none of them have so much emphasised the principle of this life being a life full of misery, as the Sâṃkhya system; none of them have defined the word "redemption" with the same precision as "the absolute cessation of pain."

On page 428 Lassen establishes a connexion between a Vedântic notion and the sentence of Plotinus, that one may also be happy when sleeping, because the soul does not sleep. But there is no necessity for it. The same doctrine appertains to the Sâṃkhya system.[1] Deep dreamless sleep is there, too, stated to be homogeneous with redemption, insomuch as in these two states the affections and functions of the inner organs have stopped, and pain with them. Considering the many cases in which the dependence of Plotinus upon the Sâṃkhya system is established, we need not hesitate to derive this idea from the Sâṃkhya system as well. These numerous agreements must, however, make us doubly careful not to expand too much the limits of this dependence; and for that reason I am bound to say that the parallels which Lassen has drawn (p. 418 et seq.) between the theory of emanation, set up by Plotinus, and the doctrine of development in the Sâṃkhya system appear to me to be out of place in the series of coincidences here treated.

Though there is a good evidence of harmony between the *pure* Sâṃkhya doctrine and the Neo-Platonism of Plotinus, there exists even a closer connexion between the latter one and *that* branch of the Sâmkhya philosophy which has assumed a theistical and ascetical character, and has, under the name of the Yoga philosophy, acquired an independent place among the Brahman systems. The morality of Plotinus is altogether of an ascetic nature. This feature might be explained, it is true, by an inclination towards Stoicism; but on account of its agreement with the Yoga system in the following points, this ascetic coloring has most probably its foundation in the influence of

1 See Sâṃkhyasûtra, V., 116.

this system. Plotinus pronounces all *worldly* things to be vain and void of value, and he therefore calls upon us to throw off the influence of the phenomenal world. If we keep off all external impressions and by way of concentration of thinking overcome the multiplicity of ideas, resulting from these impressions, the highest knowledge will fill our mind, in the form of a sudden ecstatic perception of God. There is not the slightest difference between this theory and the doctrines of the Yoga philosophy. The *ἔκστασις* of Plotinus or the *ἅπλωσις* ("the union with the deity") is the *pratibhâ* or the *prâtibham jnânam* of the Yoga system ("the immediate, universal knowledge of truth, which, after methodically exercising the ascetic Yoga-praxis, comes upon us unexpectedly").[1]

Besides Plotinus, we principally have to consider his most distinguished disciple Porphyry (from 232–304),[2] who, even more than his master, has followed the Sâṃkhya philosophy. With him the Indian influence can be proved *directly;* for he has made use of the treatise of Bardesanes, from which he copied an important passage about the Brahmans. And Bardesanes had acquired authentic information about India from the Indian ambassadors who were sent to the Emperor Antoninus Pius. In all principal points Porphyry agrees with Plotinus, as, for instance, in his demand to give up the external world and to seek

[1] See *Yogasûtra*, III., p. 33.

[2] Comp. Lassen, p. 430 et seq.

truth by contemplation; but Porphyry records in a purer way than his master the Sâṃkhya doctrine of the contrast between the spiritual and the material world. His dependency upon the Sâṃkhya philosophy is also to be noticed in his doctrines of the reign of the spiritual over the material, of the omnipresence of the soul when liberated from matter, and of the beginninglessness of the world.[1] Here we must also note the interdiction to kill animals, made by Porphyry, and his rejection of sacrifices. To be sure, Lassen says, on page 432, that Porphyry here followed the Buddhistic law; but as we are dealing with things which Buddha adopted from the Sâṃkhya system,[2] there is no reason why we should not derive them from the primary, instead of the secondary source.

I think we need not enter upon the resemblances which Lassen discovers (p. 434 et seq.) between Indian ideas and the later Neo-Platonist Abammon (about 300); for this fantastical and superstitious teacher, and the ideas peculiar to him, do not offer any but doubtful points of contact with Indian models. Only one opinion of Abammon comes into consideration, and that even was already suggested by his predecessors. It is the idea that people who are filled with a holy enthusiasm attain miraculous powers.[3] Here we clearly perceive the coincidence with

[1] This last point is not mentioned by Lassen.

[2] Compare the preface to my translation of Aniruddha's Commentary on the Sâṃkhyasûtras, etc., Calcutta, 1892.

[3] See Lassen, p. 438.

the conviction, universal in India, that miraculous powers are to be acquired by the methodical exercise of the Yoga-praxis. The Yoga philosophy promises, as the fruit of such exercise, the acquisition of the faculty of making one's self invisible, infinitely large, or infinitely light, of assuming other bodies, of changing the course of nature, and the attainment of other supernatural powers.

I cannot take leave of Neo-Platonism without mentioning a highly important point of agreement with the Indian world of thought, which, it is true, neither concerns the Sâṃkhya philosophy nor Buddhism, but which nevertheless impressively supports our arguments, as it is a most significant link in the series of Grecian loans from India. In a little essay by Professor Weber, *Vâch und λόγος, Indische Studien*, Vol. IX., the author, with great caution—"without intending in the least to settle this question"—has put forward the supposition that the Indian conception of the *vâch* (a feminine noun, meaning voice, speech, word) may have had some influence upon the idea of the λόγος which appears in Neo-Platonism and passed from there into the Gospel of St. John. Weber starts from the hymn Ṛigveda, X., 125, in which the Vâch already appears as an active power, and he refers to the personification of the "divine Vâch" or language, as the vehicle of priestly eloquence and wisdom. He then traces the development of this idea through the Brâhmaṇa literature, where the Vâch becomes more and more similar to the λόγος in the beginning of the Gospel of St. John. In the numerous passages quoted by Weber, the Vâch appears as the consort of Prajâpati, the creator, "in union with whom and by whom he accomplishes his creation; yea, the Vâch is even ultimately the most spiritual begetter, and now and then she is placed absolutely at the beginning of all things, even above the personal bearer of her own self." Weber concludes this pithy article with the following words: "There are certainly no difficulties in understanding the cosmogonical position of the Vâch which is simply to be conceived as the culmination of glorifying priestly meditation and knowledge, while the same position of the λόγος, on the other hand, appears without any suggestion as to its origin or development." This idea of Weber's I hold to be an exceedingly happy one, and, in my opinion, it deserves another name than that of a mere supposition. Only I may be allowed, in this connexion, to set one point aright. It is not Neo-Platonism in which the idea of the λόγος first appears, but it is derived there from the doctrines of Philo, which to a great extent are the basis of Neo-Platonism. Philo again adopted the λόγος doctrine from the Stoics, and they took it from Heraclitus, to whom the λόγος already was the eternal law of the course of the world.[1] My opinion, mentioned above, of Heraclitus being influenced by Indian

[1] Comp. Max Heinze, *Die Lehre vom Logos in der griechischen Philosophie*, Oldenberg, 1872.

thought, meets, accordingly, with a welcome confirmation. If the whole theory is right—and I think it is—the derivation of the λόγος theory from India must be put more than five hundred years earlier than would appear from Weber's statement.

Among the Indian doctrines which we believed we could trace in Greek philosophy, those of the Sâṃkhya system occupy the first place; agreeably to their character, they presented the smallest difficulties when transplanted to a foreign ground and embodied into a new world of thought. This influence of the Sâṃkhya and Indian philosophy in general upon Occidental philosophy does not extend beyond Neo-Platonism. And—except the Buddhistic coloring of Schopenhauer's and Hartmann's philosophy—even in our modern time we cannot notice any real influence exercised by Indian ideas. Even in the compendiums of the general history of philosophy the Indian systems are usually entirely omitted. It now need not be proved that this is a mistake. An explanation of this indifference may be found in the fact that the Indian systems became known in Europe and America only in their roughest outlines in this century, and that even now only Buddhism and two Brahman systems, Vedânta and Sâṃkhya, have been laid open to study by detailed works.

I have confined myself here to seeking out, and so far as possible, to proving the *historical* connexion between Indian and Greek philosophy. But to follow up the *internal* relations of the Indian doctrines to the whole Occidental philosophy and to trace the *occasional* agreements in detail, that would have been a task the performance of which surpasses the limits of this essay.

HINDU MONISM.

WHO WERE ITS AUTHORS, PRIESTS OR WARRIORS?

AMONG all the forms of government, class government is the worst. Carthage was governed by merchants, and the mercantile spirit of its policy finally led to the destruction of the city. Sparta was governed by warriors, and in spite of the glory of Thermopylæ it was doomed to stagnation. India was governed by priests, and the weal of the nation was sacrificed to their interests with reckless indifference. It appears that for the welfare of the community the harmonious co-operation of all classes is not only desirable but also indispensable.

Yet it is often claimed that mankind is greatly indebted to nations or states ruled by class government for having worked out the particular occupation of the ruling class to a perfection which otherwise it would not have reached. This is at least doubtful.

Carthage was eager to establish monopolies, but she contributed little to the higher development of commerce and trade among mankind.

Sparta reared brave men, but was not progressive, even in the science of war, and was worsted by so weak an adversary as Thebes. Modern strategists could learn something from Epaminondas, but little, if anything, from the Lacedæmonians.

Priestcraft has attained to a power in India unparalleled in the history of other nations, and it is no exaggeration to say that priest-rule was the ruin of the country. Yet the wisdom of the Brahmans has become proverbial. Their philosophy is praised as original and profound, and it is well known that the first monistic world-conception was thought out in ancient India. But we shall see later on what the real share of the Brahmans was in this great work.

Even in the earliest periods of Indian antiquity, as revealed to us in the songs of the Ṛigveda, we meet priests, who ventured to lay claim to the ability to make sacrifices in a manner peculiarly agreeable to the gods, and who attained to honor, wealth, and influence on account of this ability. Back into this oldest period of Indian history we can also follow the beginnings of the Indian caste system which at bottom is a product of priestly selfishness and weighs upon the Indian people like a nightmare even to the present day. However, the consolidation of the priesthood into a privileged close corporation, as well as the real development of the caste system, did not come until the time represented by the second period of Brahman literature, i. e., by the Yajurvedas, or Vedas of sacrificial formulæ, and by the Brâhmaṇas and the Sûtras, both of which present the sacrificial ritual, the former with, the latter without, theological comment. These works contain the material through which the origin of the Indian hierarchy and the caste system is clearly displayed to us. It is true, indeed, that one must often be able to read between the lines. The highest authority on this extensive literature, Professor A. Weber of Berlin, has published in the tenth volume of the *Indische Studien*, edited by him, under the title "Collectanea über die Kastenverhältnisse in den Brâhmaṇa und Sûtra," an excellent essay containing his material on this subject, and I have used it in the following pages.

With truly startling frankness the Brahmans put forth their claims in these works. In numerous passages—to begin with the most important feature—they proclaim themselves to be gods walking the earth in bodily form. "There are two sorts of gods," they say; "the real gods and the learned Brahmans who repeat the Veda;" "the Brahman represents all the divinities," indeed, "he is the god of gods," probably a unique case of its kind where clerical presumption has gone to the point of making such claims. After this we can no longer feel surprise that the Brahmans, as terrestrial gods, fancied themselves elevated far above royalty and nobility; but it might well seem surprising that kings and warriors yielded to the Brahmans the first rank in the State. In fact, however, they did it, and were obliged to do it without any reservation. From vague legends in the great Indian epic we can infer that there were bloody struggles for supremacy, in which the nobility succumbed. Accordingly these epic legends are for us an important supplement to the sources with which we are dealing.

When this struggle, which the Brahmans probably let the people proper fight out for themselves, is said to originate in the plundering by the warriors of the treasures which the priests had accumulated from the performance of sacrifices—the details are to be found in Lassen's *Indische Alterthumskunde*, second edition, I. 711—this feature of the legend is so highly probable that we are scarcely at liberty to consider it an invention, especially when we take into consideration the conditions of the time, on which we are about to throw more light. This, then, would seem to be the first attempt in history at secularisation, wherein the rulers of the time fared badly enough.

The Brahmans did not establish hierarchical concentration or ecclesiastical ranks, and wished to share personally in the government only in so far as the king was obliged to appoint a Brahman as Purohit, or household priest, who as such held also the office of prime minister. Nevertheless they were exceedingly skilful in keeping the nobility and the whole people in their power, and their chief means to this end was the higher knowledge which they claimed, especially the conduct of sacrifices. For by means of sacrifices, if rightly performed, the fulfilment of all wishes might in those times be extorted from the gods. For a scientifically presented sacrifice, which might require weeks, months, and even years, the Brahman of course demanded a fair compensation. Ten thousand cattle are prescribed as fee for a certain ceremony, for another a hundred thousand, and a later authority on ritual even demands two hundred and forty thousand for the same performance. And yet this is not the climax of priestly greed, which—to use a fitting expression of Professor Weber's—indulges in veritable orgies in these texts. When one has worked his way through the endless description of a ceremony one may read at the close the remark that the whole sacrifice is of no avail unless the fee is paid to the satisfaction of the priests. And "lest perchance —to use a modern phrase—the price be forced down by competition, the market 'beared,' it was a rule that no one might accept a fee refused by another." (Weber, p. 54.) The sacrificial ritual, so dry and wearisome for us—the only literary production of these intellectually barren centuries preceding the awakening of philosophical speculation—has such great historical significance for the very reason that it shows us the moral depravity of the Brahmans in the clearest light. To what extent sexual excesses were customary is seen from the fact that the priest is enjoined as an especial duty not to commit adultery with the wife of another during a ceremony regarded as peculiarly sacred. But any one not able to observe such continence during the period of the sacred ceremony absolves himself from all guilt by an offering of curdled milk to Varuna and Mitra!

An instructive supplement to this indulgence which the Brahmans showed for their own weaknesses, is furnished by the numerous passages in the rituals in which the officiating priest is told with perfect frankness how to proceed in the sacrifice when he wishes to do this or that injury to the man who appoints and richly pays him: in what fashion he is to deviate from the prescribed method when he wishes to deprive his employer of sight, hearing, children, property, or power. The mutual confidence which existed under these circumstances is accordingly well illustrated by a ceremony, the introduction of which before a sacrifice came to be regarded as necessary, consisting in a solemn oath by which the priest and the client bound themselves to do each other no harm knowingly during the continuance of the sacred office. After such specimens as these we shall no longer be surprised by the strange ethical conceptions which the Brahmans of this period have put on record. "Murder of any one but a Brahman is not really murder," and "a judge must always decide in favor of a Brahman as against his adversary who is not a Brahman"; such and similar things are uttered in the ritual texts with delightful coolness.

It is evident that the caste system, developed at the same time as the ritual, served chiefly to strengthen the power and influence of the priests; for when in the community the various classes are sharply distinguished from one another the priest can manage most easily to play off one factor against another to suit his own purpose. Next the Brahmans stood, as second caste, the Kshatriyas (literally the rulers, i. e., king, nobility, warriors), as third the Vaiçyas (the people proper: farmers, merchants, and artisans), while the non-Aryan, subjected aborigines, known as Çûdras, or servants, without civil or religious rights, had to fulfil the divine purpose by serving the Aryan castes, especially the Brahmans. "The Çûdra is the servant of the others, and may be cast out and killed at pleasure"; that is the humane view applied by the Brahmans to the native population.

The priestly caste might well have been content with such a condition of affairs as we find in the early Indian ritual texts. But the Brahmans were not; they continued to work steadily to secure new advantages for themselves, and to push the rigid caste distinctions to the most dreadful consequences. The result lies before us in condensed form in the famous law-book of Manu, the exact date of which is not yet ascertained, but which must have assumed its present form about the beginning of our era. The conditions which I propose to sketch briefly in the following pages were, therefore, developed in the last centuries before Christ. And even if various provisions of this law-book remained mere Brahman theory without being put into practice, enough would be left to show the social conditions of that period in a very cheerless light; and indeed it is not likely that they fell much short of the priestly ideal. Köppen, in the introductory chapter of his work on Buddhism, has estimated the social relations shown us in the laws of Manu severely but justly, saving a single error due to the exaggerated estimate of the age of the law-book prevalent at that time: he places the development of which we are speaking in the time before Buddha, whereas in fact it took place after Buddha. L. von Schröder, also, in his work *Indiens Literatur und Cultur* (Leipsic, H. Hässel, 1887) gives in the twenty-ninth lecture a clever arrangement of the material on this subject.

That the claim of the Brahmans to divine rank had not grown less with the lapse of centuries is shown by various passages of the law-book: "The Brahmans are to be revered at all times; for they are the highest divinity," indeed, "by his very descent the Brahman is a divinity to the gods themselves."

Of greater practical value for the Brahmans than this recognition as divinities must have been the numerous privileges which they enjoyed before the law. They were exempt from taxation under all circumstances, "even if the king should starve the while." Even for the worst crimes they could not be executed, chastised, or punished by confiscation of property, while the criminal code was very severe toward the other castes and especially the Çûdras. Penalties were increased in proportion as the caste of the offender was lower, and similarly fines for injuries were higher as the caste of the one offended rose. The money-lender might take from a Brahman two per cent. a month, from a Kshatriya three, from a Vaiçya four, and from a Çûdra five. And so in all provisions of the code it is evident how well the Brahmans took care of their own interests. According to this law-book the Çûdra had no rights whatever in his relations with them. "The Brahman may regard him wholly as his slave, and is therefore entitled to take away his property; for the possessions of the slave belong to his master.—The Çûdra is not to acquire wealth, even when he is in a position to do so, for this is offensive to the Brahman!" (Schröder, p. 421.)

But all these things are comparatively innocent beside the regulations whereby the Brahmans condemned to the most wretched estate innumerable human beings whose only fault was that their descent did not satisfy the conditions of the priestly scheme. In former times members of the three Aryan cactes, when they had taken as first wife a girl of their own caste, had been permitted to take additional wives from the lower castes, and the children of the latter incurred no reproach from this fact: the son of a Brahman and a Vaiçya or even a Çûdra woman was under these conditions a Brahman. But by the Laws of Manu this was no longer the case. The children of parents of unequal castes take the rank of neither father nor mother, but constitute a mixed caste, and the nature of their occupation is quite definitely prescribed in the Brahman law. As a result of this theory there arose a great number of mixed castes, all more or less despised. Moreover, the social position of many of these mixed castes was made still worse by an absurd doctrine which reduced the human race in India to the level of grass and herbs. Good seed in poor soil yields, to be sure, less increase than in good soil, but still the product is endurable. But the seed of weeds in good soil results in the strengthening and increase of the weeds. According to Brahman views, therefore, a man begets by a woman of a higher caste children of less value and rank than himself. But the lowest and most despicable human creature on earth is the child of a Çûdra and a Brahman woman. While the lot of the Çûdra was a hard one, the misery of the Chaṇḍâla, the unhappy creature born of such a union, defies all description.

"He is to dwell far from the abodes of other men, bearing marks whereby every one may recognise and avoid him; for contact with him is pollution. Only by day may he enter villages, so that he may be avoided. He is to possess only lowly animals, such as dogs and donkeys, eat only from broken dishes, dress only in garments taken from the dead, and so on. They are to do the work of executioners, every one is to shun them. The proud Brahman condemns these wretches to contempt, misery, and woe in the extreme degree." (Schröder, pp. 423, 424.)

But of course this Brahman system so fatal to all human dignity, does not end with the Chaṇḍâla; for his offspring, even if he has only a Çûdra wife, must in turn rank lower than himself. And so, in fact, there arose a great number of despised mixed castes—or rather casteless strata—each ever more despised than the other, and in turn mutually despising one another. Most varieties of these outcasts bear the names of aboriginal Indian tribes, that is to say, are thrown into the same category with particularly despised races, and in the same way are deprived of all chance for an existence befitting a human being. Even though some things that have been said about the origin of the mixed castes may be only the outcome of the Brahman passion for system, nevertheless the actual existence in India of such classes, condemned by the priesthood to a mere brute existence, is sufficiently confirmed by European observers.

The fact that in modern times the subdivisioning of the people has increased rapidly, and is still doing so to-day, so that every separate calling constitutes a distinct caste having neither social connexion with the others nor patriotic interest in them,—this fact is due at least indirectly to the influence of the Brahmans; for this melancholy condition is only a sequence and further development of the social system established by the Brahmans.

I cannot regard it as my task here to give a complete list of the Brahmans' sins; I intended only to cite enough to leave no doubt in the mind of the reader of these pages regarding the way in which the Indian priests cared for the happiness of their people. Now there will be found in general a disposition to condemn severely enough the selfishness and mercilessness of the Brahmans, but at the same time to recognise with admiration their intellectual achievements; much will be forgiven them for the sake of the profound thoughts with which they have enriched their own country and the world. It is, indeed, the "Wisdom of the Brahmans" that has given to the word India a musical sound which is perpetuated even to-day in the hearts of all to whom the endeavor after the highest truth seems to be the most important phenomenon in the development of mankind. But what will be said if it can be proven that the Brahman's profoundest wisdom, the doctrine of the All-One, which has exercised an unmistakable influence on the intellectual life of even our time, did not have its origin in the circle of Brahmans at all? Will not the scale-pan in which the Indian priesthood are being weighed rise considerably?

Before entering more in detail upon this very important question in the history of civilisation, I must briefly characterise the period in which we meet the thoughts of which I am speaking.

For centuries the Brahmans were indefatigable in devising sacrifice after sacrifice, in heaping one upon another symbolical interpretations which bear only too plainly the stamp of priestly sophistry. All at once loftier thoughts appear: traditional knowledge and the performance of sacrifices are, to be sure, not yet rejected, but the mind no longer feels satisfied by the mysteries of the "sacrificial compound," and strives toward higher and nobler goals. All minds are dominated by a passionate desire to understand the riddle of the world and to comprehend the relation of the individual to the universe. The time of deepest intellectual decline is followed by a keenly intellectual period quite filled with questionings after the Eternal-One that lies back of fluctuant phenomena and is found again in the depths of the individual being. It is the age of the Upanishads, those famous works which immediately on their appearance in Europe filled the greatest thinkers of the Occident with admiration and enthusiasm. I am speaking now only of the elder Upanishads, which originated approximately in the period from the eighth to the sixth century B. C., and not of the great mass of writings (more than two hundred in number) bearing the same name but not of equal worth, the origin of which reaches far into the Christian era. In the elder Upanishads the struggle for absolute knowledge has found an expression unique in its kind; and accordingly there is cause for rejoicing in the fact that we now have the most important of them in excellent, faithful translations from the pen of the famous Nestor of Indologians, Otto Böhtlingk. There are indeed in these Upanishads many speculations over which we shake our heads in wonder, but the meditations keep recurring to the Brahman[1],—the world-soul, the Absolute or "*Ding an sich*," or however the word so full of content may be translated,—and culminate in the thought that the Âtman, the inner self of man, is nothing less than the eternal and infinite Brahman. The language of the Upanishads is enlivened in such passages by a wonderful energy which testifies to the elevated mood in which the thinkers of that time labored to proclaim the great mystery. New phrases, figures, and similes are constantly sought in order to put into words what words are incapable of describing. For instance, the venerable Bṛihadâraṇyaka Upanishad has this: "He who dwells in the earth, but is distinct from the earth, of whom the earth knows not, whose body the earth is, who is the moving power in the earth,—this is your Self, the inner, immortal ruler." In the same words the same declaration is made regarding water, fire, ether, wind, sun, moon, and stars, of the regions of earth, of thunder and lightning, of all the worlds, of

[1]The reader will need to be alert on the distinction between Brahman (neuter) as here defined, and Brahman (masculine) meaning the priest or member of the caste. For the present meaning the spelling "Brahm" is sometimes found in English writings.—*Tr.*

all creatures and of many other things, and then the chapter closes with the words: "He who sees without being seen, hears without being heard, thinks without being thought, knows without being known, besides whom there is nothing else that sees, hears, thinks, or knows,—this is your own Self, the inner immortal ruler. All else is full of sorrow." And just after this there appears in the same famous Upanishad a knowledge-craving woman, by name Gârgî Vâchaknavî, and asks the wise Yâjnavalkya (I quote Schröder's translation with some omissions): "That which is above the sky, under the earth, and between sky and earth, which was, is, and is to be,—in what and with what is this interwoven (i. e., in what does it live and move)?" Yâjnavalkya answers evasively, or to test the intellectual powers of Gârgî: "In the ether." But Gârgî knows that this does not reach final knowledge, and asks: "But in and with what is the ether interwoven?" And Yâjnavalkya said: "That, O Gârgî, the Brahmans call the Imperishable, which is neither large nor small, neither short nor long, without connexion, without contact, without eye, without ear, without voice, without breath, without countenance, and without name. In the power of this Imperishable are maintained heaven and earth, sun and moon, day and night; subject to the power of this Imperishable, O Gârgî, some rivers flow to the east, some to the west, and in such directions as may be.

He who leaves this world, O Gârgî, without having come to know this Imperishable is to be pitied."

In the Chândogya Upanishad, a work of no less importance, the same philosophy is taught in various parables by a man named Uddâlaka to his son Çvetaketu. We find the two standing before a Nyagrodha tree, that species of fig-tree which keeps constantly sending roots to the earth from its branches, thus developing new trunks until in the course of time the one tree resembles a green hall with many pillars, capable of affording shade to hundreds, and even thousands of men. And before such a tree, the most beautiful symbol of the ever self-rejuvenating power of nature, takes place the following conversation between father and son (best rendered by Deussen, *System des Vedânta*, p. 286):

"Fetch me a fruit of the Nyagrodha tree, yonder."—"Here it is, venerable one."—"Split it."—"It is split, venerable one."—"What do you see therein?"—"I see, O venerable one, very small seeds." —"Split one of them."—"It is split, venerable one." —"What do you see therein?"—"Nothing at all, O venerable one." Then said the father: "The minute thing that you cannot see, O dear one, from this minute thing sprang this great Nyagrodha tree. Believe me, O dear one, of the same nature as this minute thing is the universe, it is the (only true) reality, it is the world-soul, it is yourself, O Çvetaketu."

This eternal foundation of all being, which every

one has within him, the absolute Being, which at the same time is identical with abstract thought, was recognised, therefore, as the only reality. The whole fluctuant multiformity of the world of phenomena is, on the other hand, a deception, an illusion (Mâyâ), a creation of ignorance. We see, it is the most consistent Monism that is here taught in the Upanishads. To have been the first in the world to proclaim this is a service that can scarcely be overestimated. But whether the merit of this belongs to the Brahmans, or is ascribed to them incorrectly, that is the question which is to be answered in the following paragraphs.

To begin with, be it observed that the closer circle of specialists: Weber, Max Müller, Deussen, Regnaud, Bhandarkar and others have for some time been pointing out evidence which suggests that another portion of the Indian people were the dominant factor in the development of the monistic doctrine in the elder Upanishads. But so far as I know the subject has not been presented to the general educated public in a popularly intelligible form.

In the second book of the Bṛihadâraṇyaka Upanishad, from which I have already quoted two specimens, occurs the following narrative, of which another and only slightly different version is preserved in the fourth book of the Kaushîtaki Upanishad:

The proud and learned Brahman Bâlâki Gârgya comes on his wanderings to Ajâtaçatru, prince of Benares, and says to him: "I will declare to you the

Brahman[1]." The king is rejoiced, and promises to reward him for it handsomely, with a thousand cows. And now the Brahman begins to deliver his wisdom: "I worship the spirit (i. e., the power) in the sun as the Brahman"; but he is interrupted by the king who tells him he already knows that and needs not to be told of it. Then the Brahman speaks of the spirit in the moon, in the lightning, in the ether, in the wind, in fire, water, and the regions of earth; but the king rejects all this as being already familiar to him. And whatever else Gârgya presents, it is nothing new to the king. Then, the story goes, the Brahman was dumb. But Ajâtaçatru asked him: "Is that all?" and Gârgya answered: "Yes, that is all." Then the king exclaimed: "These trifles do not amount to knowing the Brahman," whereupon Gârgya declares that he will become a disciple of the king and learn of him. And Ajâtaçatru replies: "It is contrary to the natural order that a Brahman receive instruction from a warrior and expect the latter to declare the Brahman to him; however, I will teach you to know it." Then the king took the Brahman by the hand and led him to where a man lay asleep. The king spoke to him; but he did not arise. But when Ajâtaçatru touched him with his hand, he rose. Now the king asked the Brahman: "Where was this man's mind, consisting as it does of knowledge, while he was asleep, and whence has it just returned?" But Gârgya could

[1] See note, p. 70.

make no reply. Then Ajâtaçatru explained to him how the mind, or the Self, of the sleeper roves in the dream, how all places belong to him, and he can be at will now a great king, now a great Brahman; but how there is then a still higher and happier state, namely, when one has fallen into a dreamless sleep, and no longer has any consciousness of anything. This is the condition in which the Self of man, unaffected by the world of phenomena, rests in its true nature, in which there is no difference between the Âtman and the Brahman.

More significant perhaps than this story is another which is reported both in the fifth book of the Chândogya Upanishad, and in the sixth book of the Bṛihadâraṇyaka Upanishad:

The young Brahman Çvetaketu comes to an assembly, and is there asked by the Prince Pravâhaṇa Jaivâli: "Young man, has your father instructed you?" —"Yes, sir."—"Do you know, then," the prince goes on, "whither creatures go from here when they die? Do you know how they return hither?" And three other questions he addresses to the Brahman youth, who is obliged to confess in confusion that he knows nothing of all these things. And so Çvetaketu returns dejected to his father, who here appears under the name of Gautama, and reproaches him: "Although you have not instructed me, you told me that you had. A simple king has addressed five questions to me, and I was unable to answer a single one." Thereupon the father answers: "My son, you know me well enough to know that I have told you all I know. Come, let us both go and become disciples of the prince." The prince receives the old Brahman with all honor, and permits him to ask for a gift. But Gautama refuses all earthly possessions, gold, cows, and horses, female slaves and robes, and desires of the prince the answers to the questions which had been addressed to his son, saying: "I come as a disciple of the revered one." Pravâhaṇa is at first disposed to put him off, but finally consents to fulfil the wish of the Brahman, and says that *no one in the world outside of the warrior caste can explain these matters.* And the following words are also significant: "*I would that neither you, O Gautama, nor any of your ancestors had part in that sin against us because of which this knowledge has until now never set up its residence among Brahmans.* To you I will reveal it; for who could refuse one who makes such an appeal?" And thereupon the king imparts to the Brahman all he knows.

The same story in all essentials is found in the beginning of the Kaushîtaki Upanishad, save that the prince has a different name, to wit, Chitra.

Passing over evidence of less importance, I will only give in condensed form the contents of the eleventh and following chapters from the fifth book of the Chândogya Upanishad, where again a man of the warrior caste, Açvapati, prince of the Kekaya, appears in possession of the highest wisdom. The book tells us that a number of very learned Brahmans, referred to by name, are meditating on the question: "What is our Self? What is the Brahman?" and they decided to go to Uddâlaka Âruni, of whom they knew that he was at the time investigating the "omnipresent Self." But he said to himself: "They will question me, and I shall not be able to answer all their questions," and therefore he invited his visitors to go with him to Açvapati, prince of the Kekayas, to request instruction from him. The king receives the visitors with honor, invites them to tarry with him, and promises them presents equal in amount to the sacrificial fees. But they said: "A man must communicate what he is occupied with. You are at present investigating the Omnipresent Self. Reveal it to us." The king replied: "I will answer you to-morrow morning." And the next forenoon, without having accepted them as disciples, i. e., without going through the formalities customary on such an occasion, he asked them one after the other: "As what do you revere the Self?" And the Brahmans made answer one after another: "As the sky, as the sun, as the ether, as water, as earth." Then the king calls attention to the fact that they are all in error, because they regard the Omnipresent Self as a single thing, existing by itself; whereas in truth it is the Infinite,—at once the infinitely small and the infinitely great.

The significance of these stories is evident. Whether real occurrences underlie the separate accounts, or whether they are to be regarded as legendary deposits of a conviction widely current at the time, cannot be determined; moreover, the question of the historical basis of these stories is of no importance for us. The fact that such tales are contained in genuinely Brahman writings which are regarded in India, and rightly so, as mainstays of Brahmanism, speaks to us in a language not to be misunderstood. It shows that the authors of the elder Upanishads did not try, or did not dare, to veil the situation that was patent in their time, and claim the monistic doctrine of the Brahman-Âtman as an inheritance of their caste; perhaps, even, that they did not consider the establishment of this doctrine as a service of such far-reaching importance as to care to claim it for the Brahman caste. In later times, it is true, this philosophy became in the fullest sense the property of the Brahmans, and has been cultivated by them for twenty-five centuries, down to the present day, so that it is still regarded as the orthodox doctrine of Brahmanism. But this does not alter the fact that it took its rise in the ranks of the warrior caste. To this caste belongs the credit of clearly recognising the hollowness of the sacrificial system and the absurdity of its symbolism, and, by opening a new world of ideas, of effecting the great revolution in the intellectual life of ancient India. When we see how the Brahmans, even after they had adopted the new doctrine, continued to cultivate the whole ceremonial system—the great milch cow of the priestly caste—and how they combined in unnatural fashion these two heterogeneous elements by representing a stage of works (ceremonials) as the indispensable prerequisite to the stage of knowledge, we are warranted in the assumption that these things developed in ancient India just as they did in the rest of the world. Intellectual enlightenment is opposed by its natural enemy, the priesthood, until it has become too strong in the people to be successfully opposed any longer. Then the priest, too, professes the new ideas, and tries to harmonise them as far as possible with his hollow shams.

But the ideas thus far treated, which are the ones most eminently characteristic of Indian wisdom, are not the only contribution by the Indian warrior caste to the thought and religion of their race. The best known of all Indians, the noble Gautama of Kapilavastu, who founded Buddhism about five hundred years before Christ, was also a Kshatriya,—according to later tradition, and formerly the only one known to us, the son of a king, but according to older sources now revealed to us chiefly through Oldenberg's meritorious labors, the son of a wealthy landholder. Buddha, "the Enlightened"—let us speak of him by this honorable title familiar to all the world—opposed most energetically the whole sacrificial system and all the prejudices of Brahmanism. The ceremonies and the priestly lore were in his eyes a cheat and a fraud, and the caste system of no force; for he taught that the highest good was just as accessible to the humblest as to the Brahman and the king; that every one without distinction of birth could attain to saving knowledge by renunciation of the world, by self-conquest, and by sacrifice of self for the good of one's fellow-creatures.

Oldenberg's excellent book on Buddha, which represents the standpoint of the latest researches, makes it unnecessary to speak in detail of the doctrines of the greatest of all Indians; only in one point, which is especially important for the connexion of our observations, I wish to present briefly my deviation from Oldenberg's views. According to the oldest sources, Buddha's method of presentation seems for the most part not adapted to the capacity of the masses; it is not popular, but abstract and philosophical. In this the inner probability seems to me to be too much against the style of these sources, which—be it not forgotten—are still some centuries later than Buddha himself. Oldenberg himself suggests a doubt whether the dry, tiresome ecclesiastical style of Buddha's alleged speeches is really a faithful reflexion of the word as first spoken. He says, p. 181: "Any one who reads the teachings which the sacred texts put into his mouth will hardly repress the question whether the form in which Buddha himself preached his doctrine can have had any resemblance to these strangely rigid shapes of abstract and often abstruse categories with their interminable repetitions. In the picture of those elder ages we dislike to think otherwise than that a strong and youthfully alert spirit animated the intercourse of master and disciples, and would therefore gladly exclude from the picture everything that would introduce the least touch of the forced and artificial." But then, after considering the conditions of the time, he concludes that it is plausible (p. 184) "that the solemnly serious style of Buddha was more closely related to the type of the speeches preserved by tradition, than to that which our sense of the natural and probable might tempt us to substitute for it?" I have not been able to convince myself of this. Such a tremendous result as followed Buddha's career was to be attained even in India only by stirring eloquence and by a popular presentation making free use of figures and parables. If Buddha had addressed himself to the understanding alone of those who stood closest to him, consisting of aristocratic elements, if he had not spoken to the hearts of the people and carried away the masses, his monastic order would scarcely have met any other fate than the other monkish communities of his time, which have vanished and left no trace, all save one. For since the doctrines of all these orders, or of their founders, were essentially alike, and since it will scarcely be attributed to accident that the teaching of Buddha alone developed into a world-religion that even to-day is the most widespread of all religions on earth, the only explanation of this is found in the assumption that Buddha's manner of teaching is responsible for the result, and that we have to seek in it the germ of the later expansion of Buddhism. Only recent investigations have refuted the once prevalent view that Buddha's appearance and career in India was a phenomenon unique in its kind, and revolutionised the contemporary social conditions of the country. In fact, Buddha was only a *primus inter pares*, one of the numerous ascetics who while seeking and teaching the means of release from the painful circuit of the transmigration of the soul, wandered about Northern India and gathered followers about them.

Only one other community founded in that time has, as above intimated, endured to the present day, that of the Jains, which has numerous members, especially in Western India. The doctrines of the Jains are so extraordinarily like those of the Buddhists that the Jains were until recently regarded as a Buddhist sect; but in fact we have to do with another religion, founded by a predecessor of Buddha named Vardhamâna Jñâtaputra—or in the language of the people, Vaddhamâna Nâtaputta—in the very same region where Buddhism arose. The only essential difference between the doctrines of the two men consists in the fact that Vardhamâna laid great stress upon castigation, while Buddha, the deeper mind of the two, declared this to be not only useless, but absolutely harmful. But the point I wish to make here is that the founder of the religion of the Jains, one that occupies a conspicuous position in the history of Indian religion and civilisation, sprang also from the warrior caste.

An entirely different character from the doctrines hitherto discussed is borne by another product of Indian intellectual life which comes within the sphere of our consideration,—a product known to most of my readers not even by name probably, yet presenting in content and development the most important problems in the history of religion: the doctrine of the Bhâgavatas or Pâncharâtras. By these names, the first being the older and original, a sect of Northern India designated itself, the existence of which is verified for the fourth century before Christ, but which in all probability reaches back into earlier, pre-Buddhist times. The Bhâgavatas professed a popular monotheism independent of ancient Brahman tradition, and worshipped the divinity under various names: Bhagavat "the Sublime"—from which word their own designation is derived—Nârâyaṇa, "Son of Man," Purushottama, "the Supreme Being," but chiefly as Kṛishṇa Vâsudeva, i. e., son of Vasudeva. This worship bore such a character that out of it was developed a feeling quite identical with the Christian feeling of believing love and devotion to God. The Indian word for this feeling is "bhakti," and for the one filled with the feeling, "bhakta." As no reliable instance of the use of the word bhakti is known from Indian literature of the pre-Christian time, or at least has yet been found, some investigators, notably Professor Weber who has won high praise for his investigation of the Kṛishṇa-cult, are inclined to regard the bhakti as borrowed from Christianity. In various publications, and especially in a highly interesting article on Kṛishṇa's birthday festival, Weber has shown that numerous Christian elements have crept into the later Kṛishṇa myths—the outward occasion for this being the similarity in sound of the names Kṛishṇa and Christus—: the accounts of the birth of Christ among the shepherds, of the stable, of the manger as his birth-place, and many other features of this sort. Nevertheless I cannot adopt the opinion that the bhakti was transplanted from a foreign land into the exceedingly fertile soil of the realm of Indian thought, because its earliest appearance is in a time for which in my opinion Christian influences in India have not yet been demonstrated. As a detailed discussion of this very interesting question is not possible without the introduction of all sorts of erudite material, I must in this place limit myself to the observation that for one who is intimate with the intellectual life of ancient India the doctrine of the bhakti is entirely conceivable as a genuine product of India. Not only are monotheistic ideas demonstrable in India for the earliest antiquity, but the Indian folk-soul has always been marked by a powerful aspiration for the Divine—and especially so in the times we are here considering—so that we need not be surprised if this intensely ardent trait expresses itself, in a popular religion not resting on a philosophical basis, as devotion to God and love for God. The founder of this religion was Kṛishṇa Vâsudeva, who, though later raised to the rank of a god, or better, identified with God, was, as his name and the legends attached to it indicated, *a member of the warrior caste.* As early as in the Mahâbhârata, the great Indian national epic, Brahmanism has appropriated the person and doctrine of Kṛishṇa, and made of the deified hero a form of the god Vishṇu. Thus in this case also Brahmanism managed to renew its own vitality by appropriating an originally un-Brahmanic element.

So we have seen that neither the profound Monism of the Upanishads, nor the highly moral religions of the Buddhists and the Jains, nor, finally, the faith of the Bhâgavatas, founded in pure devotion to God, was originated in the Indian priestly caste. However favorably one may judge of the achievements accomplished by the Brahmans during the course of time in the most varied fields of knowledge—and I myself would be far from wishing to belittle their services—this much at least is established, that the greatest intellectual performances, or rather almost all the performances of significance for mankind, in India, have been achieved by men of the warrior caste.

INDEX.

CATALOGUE OF PUBLICATIONS

OF THE

OPEN COURT PUBLISHING CO.

COPE, E. D.

THE PRIMARY FACTORS OF ORGANIC EVOLUTION.
121 cuts. Pp., xvi, 547. Cloth, $2.00, net.

MÜLLER, F. MAX.

THREE INTRODUCTORY LECTURES ON THE SCIENCE OF THOUGHT.
With a correspondence on "Thought Without Words," between F. Max Müller and Francis Galton, the Duke of Argyll, George J. Romanes and others. 128 pages. Cloth, 75 cents. Paper, 25 cents.

THREE LECTURES ON THE SCIENCE OF LANGUAGE.
The Oxford University Extension Lectures, with a Supplement, "My Predecessors." 112 pages. 2nd Edition. Cloth, 75 cents. Paper, 25c.

ROMANES, GEORGE JOHN.

DARWIN AND AFTER DARWIN.
An Exposition of the Darwinian Theory and a Discussion of Post-Darwinian Questions. Two Vols., $3.00. Singly, as follows:
1. The Darwinian Theory. 460 pages. 125 illustrations. Cloth, $2.00.
2. Post-Darwinian Questions. Ed. by C. L. Morgan. Pp. 338. Cl. $1.50.

AN EXAMINATION OF WEISMANNISM.
236 pages. Cloth, $1.00. Paper, 35c.

THOUGHTS ON RELIGION.
Edited by Charles Gore, M. A., Canon of Westminster. Third Edition Pages, 184. Cloth, gilt top, $1.25.

RIBOT, TH.

THE PSYCHOLOGY OF ATTENTION.
THE DISEASES OF PERSONALITY.
THE DISEASES OF THE WILL.
Authorised translations. Cloth, 75 cents each. Paper, 25 cents. *Full set, cloth, $1.75, net.*

MACH, ERNST.

THE SCIENCE OF MECHANICS.
A Critical and Historical Exposition of its Principles. Translated by T. J. McCormack. 250 cuts. 534 pages. ½ m., gilt top. $2.50.

POPULAR SCIENTIFIC LECTURES.
313 pages. 44 cuts. Cloth, gilt top. Net, $1.00.

THE ANALYSIS OF THE SENSATIONS.
Pp. 208. Cloth, $1.25, net.

GOODWIN, REV. T. A.

LOVERS THREE THOUSAND YEARS AGO.
As Indicated by the Song of Solomon. Pp. 41. Boards, 50c.

HOLYOAKE, G. J.

ENGLISH SECULARISM. A Confession of Belief.
Pp. 146. Cloth, 50c., net.

CORNILL, CARL HEINRICH.

THE PROPHETS OF ISRAEL.
Popular Sketches from Old Testament History. Pp., 200. Cloth, $1.00

THE RISE OF THE PEOPLE OF ISRAEL.
See *Epitomes of Three Sciences*, below.

BINET, ALFRED.

THE PSYCHIC LIFE OF MICRO-ORGANISMS.
Authorised translation. 135 pages. Cloth, 75 cents; Paper, 25 cents.

ON DOUBLE CONSCIOUSNESS.
Studies in Experimental Psychology. 93 pages. Paper, 15 cents.

TOLSTOI, COUNT LEO.

CHRISTIANITY AND PATRIOTISM.
In preparation.

WAGNER, RICHARD.

A PILGRIMAGE TO BEETHOVEN.
A Novelette. Frontispiece, portrait of Beethoven. Pp. 40. Boards, 50c

WEISMANN, AUGUST.

GERMINAL SELECTION. AS A SOURCE OF DEFINITE VARIATION.
Pp. 73. Paper, 25c.

NOIRÉ, LUDWIG.

ON THE ORIGIN OF LANGUAGE. Pp. 57. Paper, 15c.

FREYTAG, GUSTAV.

THE LOST MANUSCRIPT. A Novel.
2 vols. 953 pages. Extra cloth, $4.00. One vol., cl., $1.00; paper, 75c

MARTIN LUTHER.
Illustrated. Pp. 130. Cloth, $1.00.

HERING, EWALD.

ON MEMORY, and THE SPECIFIC ENERGIES OF THE NERVOUS SYSTEM. Pp. 50. Paper, 15c.

TRUMBULL, M. M.

THE FREE TRADE STRUGGLE IN ENGLAND.
Second Edition. 296 pages. Cloth, 75 cents; paper, 25 cents.

WHEELBARROW: ARTICLES AND DISCUSSIONS ON THE LABOR QUESTION
With portrait of the author. 303 pages. Cloth, $1.00; paper, 35 cents

EARL GREY ON RECIPROCITY AND CIVIL SERVICE REFORM.
With Comments by Gen. M. M. Trumbull. Price, 10 cents.

GOETHE AND SCHILLER'S XENIONS.

Selected and translated by Paul Carus. Album form. Pp., 162. Cl., $1.00

OLDENBERG, H.

ANCIENT INDIA: ITS LANGUAGE AND RELIGIONS.
Pp. 100. Cloth, 50c. Paper, 25c.

CARUS, PAUL.

THE ETHICAL PROBLEM.
90 pages. Cloth, 50 cents; Paper, 30 cents.

FUNDAMENTAL PROBLEMS.
Second edition, enlarged and revised. 372 pp. Cl., $1.50. Paper, 50c.

HOMILIES OF SCIENCE.
317 pages. Cloth, Gilt Top, $1.50.

THE IDEA OF GOD.
Fourth edition. 32 pages. Paper, 15 cents.

THE SOUL OF MAN.
With 152 cuts and diagrams. 458 pages. Cloth, $3.00.

TRUTH IN FICTION. TWELVE TALES WITH A MORAL.
Fine laid paper, white and gold binding, gilt edges. Pp. 111. $1.00

THE RELIGION OF SCIENCE.
Second, extra edition. Price, 50 cents. R. S. L. edition, 25c. Pp. 103

PRIMER OF PHILOSOPHY.
240 pages. Second Edition. Cloth, $1.00. Paper, 25c.

THE PHILOSOPHY OF THE TOOL.
Pages, 24. Paper, illustrated cover, 10c.

OUR NEED OF PHILOSOPHY.
Pages, 14. Paper, 5c.

SCIENCE A RELIGIOUS REVELATION.
Pages, 21. Paper, 5c.

THE GOSPEL OF BUDDHA. According to Old Records.
4th Edition. Pp., 275. Cloth, $1.00. Paper, 35 cents. In German, $1.25.

KARMA. A STORY OF EARLY BUDDHISM.
Illustrated by Japanese artists. 2nd Edition. Crêpe paper, 75 cents.

GARBE, RICHARD.

THE REDEMPTION OF THE BRAHMAN. A TALE OF HINDU LIFE.
Laid paper. Gilt top. 96 pages. Price, 75c. Paper, 25c.

THE PHILOSOPHY OF ANCIENT INDIA.
Pp. 89. Cloth, 50c. Paper, 25c.

EPITOMES OF THREE SCIENCES.

1. THE STUDY OF SANSKRIT. By *H. Oldenberg.* 2. EXPERIMENTAL PSYCHOLOGY. By *Joseph Jastrow.* 3. THE RISE OF THE PEOPLE OF ISRAEL. By *C. H. Cornill.* 140 pages. Cloth, reduced to 50 cents.

The Religion of Science Library.

A collection of bi-monthly publications, most of which are reprints o books published by The Open Court Publishing Company. Yearly, $1.50 Separate copies according to prices quoted. The books are printed upon good paper, from large type.

The Religion of Science Library, by its extraordinarily reasonable price will place a large number of valuable books within the reach of all readers

The following have already appeared in the series:

No. 1. *The Religion of Science.* By PAUL CARUS. 25c.
2. *Three Introductory Lectures on the Science of Thought.* By F. MAX MÜLLER. 25c.
3. *Three Lectures on the Science of Language.* By F. MAX MÜLLER. 25c.
4. *The Diseases of Personality.* By TH. RIBOT. 25c.
5. *The Psychology of Attention.* By TH. RIBOT. 25c.
6. *The Psychic Life of Micro-Organisms.* By ALFRED BINET. 25c.
7. *The Nature of the State.* By PAUL CARUS. 15c.
8. *On Double Consciousness.* By ALFRED BINET. 15c.
9. *Fundamental Problems.* By PAUL CARUS. 50c.
10. *The Diseases of the Will.* By TH. RIBOT. 25c.
11. *The Origin of Language.* By LUDWIG NOIRE. 15c.
12. *The Free Trade Struggle in England.* By M. M. TRUMBULL. 25c.
13. *Wheelbarrow on the Labor Question.* By M. M. TRUMBULL. 35c.
14. *The Gospel of Buddha.* By PAUL CARUS. 35c.
15. *The Primer of Philosophy.* By PAUL CARUS. 25c.
16. *On Memory,* and *The Specific Energies of the Nervous System.* By PROF EWALD HERING. 15c.
17. *The Redemption of the Brahman.* A Tale of Hindu Life. By RICHARD GARBE. 25c.
18. *An Examination of Weismannism.* By G. J. ROMANES. 35c.
19. *On Germinal Selection.* By AUGUST WEISMANN. 25c.
20. *Lovers Three Thousand Years Ago.* By T. A. GOODWIN. 15c.
21. *Popular Scientific Lectures.* By ERNST MACH. 35c.
22. *Ancient India : Its Language and Religions.* By H. OLDENBERG. 25c
23. *The Prophets of Ancient Israel.* By PROF. C. H. CORNILL. 25c.
24. *Homilies of Science.* By PAUL CARUS. 35c.
25. *Thoughts on Religion.* By G. J. ROMANES. 50 cents.
26. *The Philosophy of Ancient India.* By PROF. RICHARD GARBE. 25c.

Published by

Facsimile Publisher
Ashok Vihar, Delhi-110052 (India)
Website: www.facsimilepublishers.com

Distributed by

Gyan Books Pvt. Ltd.
5, Ansari Road, Daryaganj, New Delhi-110002 (India)
E-mail: books@gyanbooks.com, Website: www.gyanbooks.com

8 888000 991250